Use It! Don't Lose It!

ALGEBRA
Daily Skills Practice

by John Linton

IncentivePublications

BY WORLD BOOK
a Scott Fetzer company

Illustrated by Kathleen Bullock
Cover by Geoffrey Brittingham

Print Edition ISBN 978-0-86530-668-4
E-book Edition ISBN 978-1-62950-056-0 (PDF)

World Book, Inc.
180 North LaSalle Street
Suite 900
Chicago, Illinois 60601
U.S.A.

For information about World Book and Incentive Publications products, **call 1-800-967-5325,** or visit our websites at **www.worldbook.com** and **www.incentivepublications.com.**

Printed in the United States of America by Integrated Books International, Dulles, Virginia

Don't let those algebra skills get lost or rusty!

As a teacher you work hard to teach algebra skills and concepts to your students. Your students work hard to understand and master them. Do you worry that they will forget the material as you move on to the next concept?

If so, here's a plan for you and your students—one that will keep those algebra skills sharp.

Use It! Don't Lose It! provides daily algebra practice for all the basic skills, concepts, and processes. There are five problems a day, every day for 36 weeks. The skills and concepts match the basic curriculum for an Algebra I course, and are correlated to national and state standards.

Students practice all the algebra skills, concepts, and processes in a spiraling sequence. The plan starts with the simplest level of algebra skills, progressing gradually to higher-level tasks, as it continually circles around and back to the the same skills at a little higher level, again and again. Each time a skill shows up, it has a new context— requiring students to dig into their memories, recall what they know, and apply it to another situation.

Contents

How to Use Daily Skills Practice

To get started, reproduce each page, slice the Monday–Thursday lesson pages in half, or prepare a transparency. The lessons can be used . . .

- **for independent practice**—Reproduce the lessons and let students work individually or in pairs to practice skills at the beginning or end of a math class.
- **for small group work**—Students can discuss and solve the problems together and agree on answers.
- **for the whole class review**—Make a transparency and work through the problems together as a class.

Helpful Hints for Getting Started

- Though students may work alone on the items, always find a way to review and discuss the answers together. In each review, ask students to describe how they solved the word problems or other problems that involve choices of strategies.

- Allow more time for the Friday lesson. The Challenge Problem may take longer than any other problem of the week. Students can work in small groups to discover good strategies and correct answers for this problem.

- Decide ahead of time about the use of calculators. Many of these problems are the kinds that are ordinarily done with a good graphing calculator. Let students know which lessons or specific items are approved for calculator assistance!

- There will not always be room for students to solve the problems on the page. Have scratch paper available for students at all times.

- The daily lessons are designed to be completed in a short time period, so that they can be used along with your regular daily instruction. However, don't end the discussion until you are sure all students "get it," or at least until you know which ones don't get something and will need extra instruction. This will strengthen all the other work students do in algebra class.

- Keep a consistent focus on the strategies and processes for problem solving. Encourage students to explore and share different approaches for solving the problems. Explaining (orally or in writing) their problem-solving process is an important math skill. Be open to answers (correct ones, of course) that are not supplied in the Answer Key.

- Take note of which items leave some or all of the students confused or uncertain. This will alert you to which skills need more instruction.

- The daily lessons may include some skills or concepts your students have not yet learned. In these cases, students may skip items. Or, you might encourage them to consider how the problem could be solved. Or, you might use the occasion for a short lesson that would get them started on this skill.

1. Global online music sales have exploded. It was expected that music lovers would spend $2 billion for online music in 2007.

In scientific notation, this number is:

○ 2×10^6 ○ 2.2×10^7

○ 2^9 ● 2×10^9 *2000000000*

○ 2.2×10^8 ○ 2×10^{10}

2. Solve: **$6x = -30$**

$x = -5$

3. Why is **$15 = \frac{x}{3}$** called an *equation*?

an equation has an equal sign w/ two sides to it.

4. Write these in order from least to greatest:

-3.1 $\frac{7}{8}$ *.875*   0.31   -5   *$-5, -3.1, 0.31, \frac{7}{8}$*

0   11.5   -12 2^3 *8* $\sqrt{16}$ *4*

$-12, 0, \sqrt{16}, 2^3, 11.5$

5. At the 48th Annual Grammy Awards Show (in 2005), awards were given in 110 different categories.

ALBUM OF THE YEAR

BEST ROCK ALBUM

SONG OF THE YEAR

BEST ROCK PERFORMANCE BY A GROUP

BEST ROCK SONG

WRITERS OR SINGERS FROM THE GROUP U2 WON GRAMMIES IN FIVE CATEGORIES.

IN WHAT PERCENT OF THE CATEGORIES DID U2 WIN AWARDS?

about 5%

GRAMMY U2

$\frac{5}{110} = \frac{x}{100}$

$\frac{500 = 110x}{110}$

$x =$

1. Use words to write this expression:

$9 + 7x$

nine plus seven times x

2. In 1998, Rapper Revel XD set a record by speaking 683 syllables in 54.501 seconds. The number that represents this amount of time is:

(**a rational number**)

an irrational number

a whole number

3. Solve for x with y = 6.

$x + 2(6) = 17$ **$x + 2y = 17$**

$x + 12 = 17$

$x = 5$

4. Identify the base in each expression.

x^5   **y^{10}**   **5^2**   **2^3**

x   *y*   *5*   *2*

5. The dot frequency diagram shows the number of songs a band rehearsed every week for 25 weeks. Each dot stands for one week.

a. During how many weeks did the band rehearse more than five songs? *15*

b. What is the mean (average) number of songs rehearsed per week? *9*

AVERAGE NUMBER OF SONGS REHEARSED

Weeks

0 1 2 3 4 5 6 7 8 9 10

songs

1. Ryan heard that the shortest music video ever made is just 2.18 seconds long. Use words to write this number.

> two and eighteen hundredths

2. Simplify: $6 + 12 - (4 + n)$

$18 - (4+n)$

$14 + n$

3. Explain the rule for multiplying two exponential expressions that have the same base.

> add the two different exponents and apply the sum to the same base

4. Is the equation solved correctly?

$-16 = y$

$-16 + y = 2y$

no $y = -8$

5. Ryan is a drummer in a five-member percussion group. He had the name of the group embossed on his new drum.

Another member of the group draws a letter of the alphabet at random. What is the probability that the letter drawn will be a letter in the name of the group?

$\frac{8}{26}$ or $\frac{4}{13}$

1. Write T (true) or F (false) for each sentence.

a. _+_ $2 + 5 > -5$ d. _f_ $0 < -6$

b. _f_ $12 < 12$ e. _+_ $7 > -12$

c. _f_ $8 < 5$ f. _f_ $4^3 = 12$
                        64

2. Evaluate the expression if **x = 7** and **y = 12**.

5x – y

$5(7) - 12$

$35 - 12$ ⟨23⟩

3. Write this number:

negative twelve and twelve thousandths -12.012

4. Subtract: $\sqrt{121} - \sqrt{64}$

$11 - 8$

3

5. The rock band Van Halen required a supply of M&Ms to be provided backstage. They asked to have the brown ones removed.

Assume that a host at one concert started with an equal number of six colors of M&Ms (red, orange, yellow, brown, green, blue). After removing the brown candies, she had 725 M&Ms left to put into the bowl. How many brown M&Ms were removed? $5b = 725$

Write and solve an equation to find the answer.

145

1. Write the number that is the opposite of the one found on the sign.

JAZZ ARENA
SECTION 15

−15

2. In 2006, 40% of U.S. Internet users bought music online. This number was 70,800,000 buyers. Use the equation to find out how many Internet users there were in the U.S. in 2006.

$\frac{4}{10}x = 70{,}800{,}000 \times \frac{10}{4}$

$x = 177{,}000{,}000$

3. Solve for n: $n + 7 - 4n = -8$

Circle the correct answer.

n = 8   (n = 5)   n = −5   n = −8

$n - 4n = -15$
$-3n = -15$
$n = 5$

4. Draw a stem on the musical note. It should connect these points: (−1, 2); (0, 3); (2, 5); (3, 6)

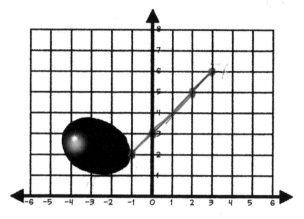

5. Challenge Problem

The Lost Tooth Band has five members of different ages: JoJo, Damon, Samantha, Will, and Brandy. The total of their ages is 121.

Will is three-fourths of JoJo's age.
Brandy is one year older than twice Damon's age.
Samantha is eight years older than JoJo.
JoJo is four times the age of Damon.

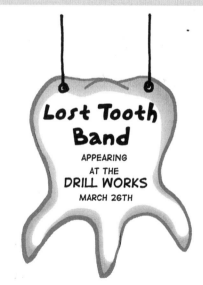

Lost Tooth Band APPEARING AT THE DRILL WORKS MARCH 26TH

Which equation will help you find Damon's age?

a. $d + (2d + 1) + 4d + 8 + \frac{3}{4} + d = 121$

b. $d + (2d + 1) + 4d + (4d + 8) + \frac{3}{4}(4d) = 121$

Find the age for each band member.

_____ _____ _____ _____ _____

1. Solve the equation for x. The solution shows the number of barrels of buried pirate gold found on Crusoe Island in 2005.

$$20x - 300 - 7x + 500 = 8000$$

$13x + 200 = 8000$

2. Evaluate x^5 for $x = 2$. $13x = 7800$

㉜

2^5 $2 \cdot 2 \cdot 2 \cdot 2 \cdot 2$ $x = 600$

$8 \cdot 2 \cdot 2$
$8 \cdot 4$

3.

> **3.** When a ship was sinking, some sailors threw a valuable treasure chest overboard. The deck of the ship was **46** feet above the water's surface. The chest sank to a depth of **387** feet (**-387**).
>
> Write and solve a subtraction equation to find the difference between the two locations. $x = 387 - 46$

4. Write this expression in words:

$$18 \cdot (a - b)$$

eighteen times a minus b

5. Back in 1882, a blacksmith from a wild west Arizona town robbed stagecoaches in his spare time. He hid a large sum of money that was never found. The dollar amount is believed to be   69,000

6.9×10^4.

Write this amount in standard notation.

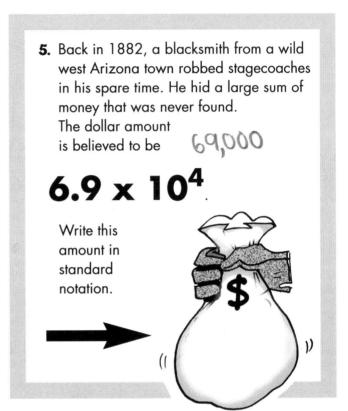

1. Which sentence does NOT show an inequality?
- a) **a** plus **b** is approximately equal to **c** plus **b**.
- b) The product of **a** and **b** is equal to half of **d**.
- c) The difference between **n** and **m** is equal to or greater than four **p**.

2. Solve for b if a = –4.

$$a - 6 - b = -15$$

$-4 - 6 - b = -15$
$-10 - b = -15$
$-b = -5$
$b = 5$

3. Which is greater?

$4\sqrt{16}$ OR $3\sqrt{25}$

2

4. The number represented shows the location (in feet) of treasure found from the 1869 sunken ship, the *Abbatucci*. What is the absolute value of the number?

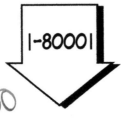

$|-8000|$

8000

5. Examine the graph that shows the kinds of treasures recovered from a sunken ship. What percent of the total value came from the emeralds?

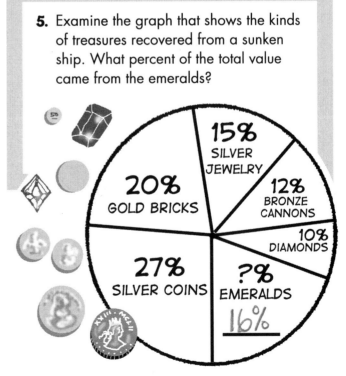

15% SILVER JEWELRY

20% GOLD BRICKS

12% BRONZE CANNONS

10% DIAMONDS

27% SILVER COINS

?% EMERALDS   16%

1. Which equation is solved correctly?

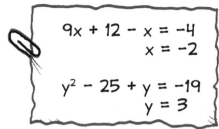

$$9x + 12 - x = -4$$
$$x = -2$$

$$y^2 - 25 + y = -19$$
$$y = 3$$

2. Do the two versions of the expression match?

six times the sum of negative twelve and another number subtracted from fifty

$$50 - 6(-12 + x)$$

3. Simplify: d^3d^5

4. What operation should be done first when finding this solution?

$$\sqrt{64} + 92 - (12 + 8) =$$

5. In 1622, a fleet of Spanish ships was lost near Cuba. In 1986, treasure hunters recovered one million dollars worth of gold and silver from the sunken ships in four days. Assuming that they could continue to find treasure at that same rate, how much could be found in a full week (in dollar value)?

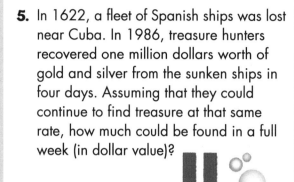

HOW MANY DOLLARS?

_____

1. Old stories claim that a large sum of money was supposedly stashed long ago near Bumble Bee, Arizona. The rumored amount of this treasure is a number that is $45 thousand less than one-eighth of a million dollars. What is the amount?

2. Name the two square roots of 25.

WOW!

3. Evaluate if $a = -4$ and $b = 3$.

$$6a + b + 8b$$

4. Write three different possible solutions:

$$2x \leq 15$$

A ☐ B ☐ C ☐

5. Write T (true) or F (false) for each statement.

____ Zero has no square roots.

____ Every positive number has exactly two real square roots.

____ Every negative number has no real square roots.

____ The number 200 has a whole number square root.

____ The number ONE has no square roots.

____ The radicand in the following is 9.

$$\sqrt{81}$$

1. Solve: $\frac{2x}{3} = 12$

2. Which property is demonstrated?

$$4x(x + 12) = 4x^2 + 48x$$

3. Complete the next three flags.

4. Bank robber John Dillinger supposedly buried $200,000 in a Wisconsin field in 1933. Four friends searching for the treasure agreed to split it this way: Zach would get $\frac{1}{5}$ of the total. Rhonda would get $\frac{1}{4}$ of what remained after Zach got his share. Sue and Damian would share the rest. If they find the treasure, how much will Sue's share be?

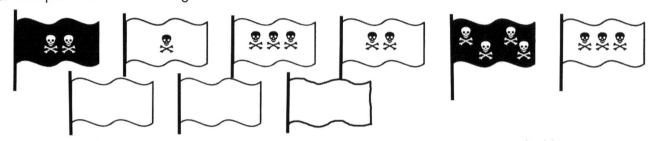

5. Challenge Problem

A treasure hunter lands at point A on the island. He hikes to each of the locations shown by the coordinates (below) and digs for treasure at each spot. Draw his trail from one point to the next, in the order given. Draw an **X** each place he digs. He finds the treasure at the last location.

Draw a treasure chest there.

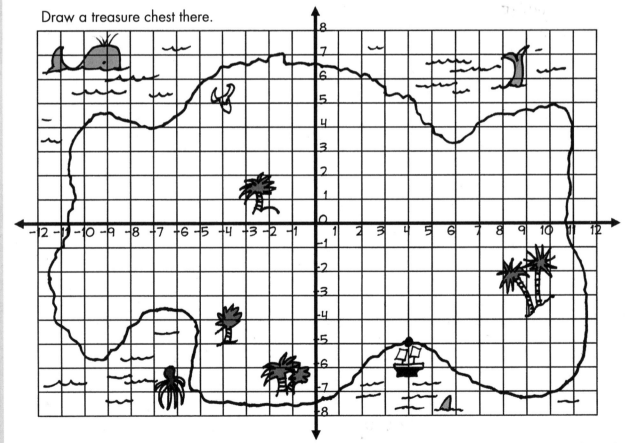

(4, −2); (0, −4); (−4, −5); (0, −2); (2, 4); (−9, 2); (−9, −3); (0, 0); (8, 0); (10, 2); (10, −5); (7, −3)

1. This equation, when solved, will give the number of gallons of water a hippo can drink in 24 hours. Use numbers and symbols to write the equation.

> The difference between three times a number and the sum of twelve squared plus ninety-two equals five hundred fourteen.

$$3x - (12^2 + 92) = 514$$

2. Give the reciprocal of $\frac{5}{6}$. $\frac{6}{5}$

3. Which has the greatest value?

$$4^3 \quad \boxed{3^5} \quad 2^6 \quad 5^3$$

64   243   64   125

4. Read the signs in example # 5.

Three of these animals flapped their wings continuously for a minute, resulting in 49,200 flaps. Which insect was not included?

gnat

5. Read the signs. Answer the questions.

a. What is the mean number of flaps per second for the four insects?

455
1,820 ÷ 4

b. If all four insects flap continuously for two minutes, how many wing flaps will result?

218,400

GNAT
FLAPS WINGS
1000 TIMES PER SECOND
120,000
60,000

HORSEFLY
FLAPS WINGS
200 TIMES PER SECOND
12,000
24,000

DRAGONFLY
FLAPS WINGS
20 TIMES PER SECOND
1,200
2,400

MOSQUITO
FLAPS WINGS
600 TIMES PER SECOND
36000
72,000

1. Finish the sentence:

The product of two negative numbers is a _positive_ **number.**

2. Evaluate: $7(\sqrt{81})$

63

3. Write an expression to match the words:

the sum of four times a number (x) and twice the square of another number (y)

$$4x + 2y^2$$

4. A trout swims one and two-third miles in 25 minutes. Solve the proportion to find out how far the trout can swim in one hour.

$$\frac{\frac{5}{3}}{25} = \frac{x}{60}$$

$$25x = 100$$
$$x = 4$$

4 miles

5. In 1997, a dog named Brutus set an interesting record. He became the world's highest sky diving dog when he descended a distance of 4,572 feet (wearing a parachute, of course). A second skydiving dog jumped a shorter distance (d). A third dog jumped one-third the distance of the second dog. Together their dives equaled Brutus's distance. How far did the second dog jump?

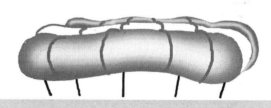

$$\frac{1}{3}d = 4,572 - d$$
$$\frac{7}{3}d = 4,572$$
$$d = 1959$$

WEDNESDAY WEEK 3 _____ MATH PRACTICE
Name

1.

THE SOLUTION IS X = 2.
WHAT IS THE EQUATION? (CIRCLE IT.)

$\frac{1}{3}x = 6$ $\boxed{\frac{4x}{2x} = 8}$

$\frac{1}{4}x = \frac{1}{2}$ $\frac{3}{2}x - 6 = 0$

BUMBLE BEE,
ARIZONA,
OR BUST!

2. Add: $(4 + 7x) + (9x - x^2 - 20)$

$-16 + 15x - x^2$

3. Explain the rule for dividing exponential expressions if the bases are the same.

subtract the exponents

4. Simplify:

$6 + 10d^2 + d^2 - 12 < 40 + d$

$-6 + 11d^2 < 40 + d$

5. There is enough energy in one gallon of nectar for a bee to travel four million miles at seven miles per hour.

571,429 hrs

Assuming that a bee does this, how much travel time would it take?

(Use the formula $rt = d$*. Round your answer to the nearest whole number.)*

$7t = 4,000,000$
$t = 571,429$

THURSDAY WEEK 3 _____ MATH PRACTICE
Name

1. $2xy^2 + 6x - 8x$

Is this a correct factoring for the above expression?

$(2x)(y^2 + 3 - 4)$

2. Evaluate for $x = -6$ and $y = 3$.

$\boxed{60}$ $\frac{5x^2}{y}$ $\frac{5 \cdot -6^2}{3} = \frac{180}{3}$

3. When you graph a linear inequality, how do you decide if the circle on the number line is shaded or not shaded?

if the number is less/greater than or equal to the other, it's shaded.

4. Charlie was asked to evaluate an expression. Did he do it correctly?

$\sqrt{4^2 + 3^2} = 36$

$\sqrt{4^2 + 3^2} = 5$

NO

5. In response to a survey, seven percent of cat owners in the U.S. reported that their cats snore. If the number of snoring cats is 4,606,000, what is the total number of cats in the U.S.?

65,800,000

Which equation will find the answer to the question? *(c = total number of cats)*

$(4,606,000)(0.07) = c$
$4,606,000c = 0.07$
$\boxed{0.07c = 4,606,000}$

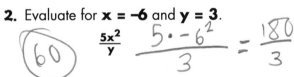

$\frac{7}{100} = \frac{4,606,000}{x}$

$0.07c = 4,606000$
$c = 65,800,000$ $460,600,000$

Use It! Don't Lose It! IP 613-4   **12**   ©Incentive Publications, Inc., Nashville, TN

1. A baby bird can eat 14 feet of earthworm every day. At this rate, how many days would it take six baby birds to eat 840 feet of worms?

2. Let **t** represent the lifespan of a tarantula. Let **r** = the lifespan of a rhinoceros. Use the two equations to find both life spans.

$$t = (\tfrac{1}{2}r) - 10 \qquad t + r = 80$$

3. Evaluate: **(–2) (15) (–10) (–3) =**

4. Is this a graph of the following equation?

$$x = y + 1$$

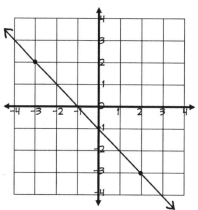

5. Challenge Problem

Use information from the table to answer the questions.

   a. **5.2 x 10³ noses**—How many slugs?

   b. **1.6 x 10⁴ brains**—How many leeches?

Write answers in scientific notation.

   c. **A hive of 53,000 bees**— How many wings?

   d. **A school of 8,750 catfish**— How many taste buds?

   e. **A bay of 5,290 scallops**— How many eyes?

   f. **A river with 11,200 alligators**— How many teeth?

   g. **A meadow with 492 porcupines**— How many quills?

   h. **A tent with 350 mosquitoes**— How many teeth?

Curious Animal Facts

PORCUPINE	30,000 QUILLS
MOSQUITO	47 TEETH
SCALLOP	100 EYES
ALLIGATOR	80 TEETH
CATFISH	100,000 TASTE BUDS
LEECH	32 BRAINS
SLUG	4 NOSES
BEE	4 WINGS

1. In 1985, Nike released the *Air Jordan I* athletic shoe. Evaluate the expression below to find the amount of sales (in dollars) of these shoes in the first year.

$$10^5 \cdot 10^2 \sqrt{169}$$

2. Write this number in words: **101.0101**

3. Solve: $\frac{88}{n} = 30 - 41$

4. Members of a tennis team wore out three pairs of shoes in a year. Cross-country runners wore out four pairs a year. Which expression represents the total shoes worn out in a year?

(t = # of tennis players,
r = # of cross-country runners)

   $7(r + t)$ $(r + t)(3)(4)$

   $4r + 3t$ $7(r - t)$

5. For each of these subsets of the real number system, give a description and an example.

integers
example:
description:

whole numbers
example:
description:

rational numbers
example:
description:

irrational numbers
example:
description:

1. Solve: $2x^2 + 4 = x^2 + 29$

2. Mom's shoofly pie has a diameter of nine inches. She cuts it into eight equal pieces and serves one to me. What is the measurement of the outside rounded edge of my slice?

3. Write in order from least to greatest.

  -7 $\sqrt[3]{-27}$ 77

  0.7 -7.7 $(-7)^2$

4. Evaluate each expression.

$$\sqrt[3]{125}$$

$$\sqrt{484}$$

$$\sqrt[6]{64}$$

5. Abby creates a shoebox by folding the pattern below on dotted lines and gluing or taping the corners. Write a formula and use it to find the volume of the box.

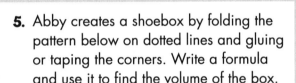

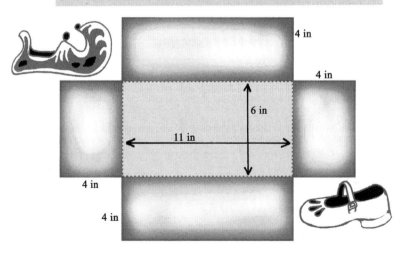

4 in

4 in

6 in

11 in

4 in

4 in

1. A group of students made a chain of shoelaces and strung it around the perimeter of a football field (120 yd long, 53 yd wide). They calculated the perimeter of the field to be 293 yards. Were they correct?

2. What is the second operation to be performed in evaluating the expression?

$$\sqrt{961} + y^2 - (6y - 2y)$$

3. The world's largest sandal has a width that is 2.47 meters less than its length. Write an expression to show this comparison.

4. Circle the correct simplification of $\dfrac{n^{12}}{n^2}$.

   n^6 n^{14} n^{10} n^{24}

5. A farrier puts new shoes on a horse named Pablo. The farrier is five years older than three times the age of the horse. The sum of their ages is 33.

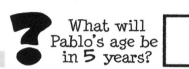
What will Pablo's age be in 5 years?

Explain your solution:

1. Evaluate: $\sqrt[3]{-216}$

2. When the world record was set for the most participants wearing Wellington boots in a race, the number was surprisingly large. The expression will help you find that number.

$$3^2(90 + 19)$$

3. Evaluate for $p = \dfrac{1}{5}$.

$$p^2 + 5 - 1\dfrac{1}{25}$$

4. In a horseshoe-tossing tournament, Louis had five tosses, totaling 1,866 feet. The first three were 274 feet, 316 feet, and 250 feet. The last two tosses were the same. What was the distance of his fifth toss?

5. Place the following numbers correctly into the sets shown below in the diagram.

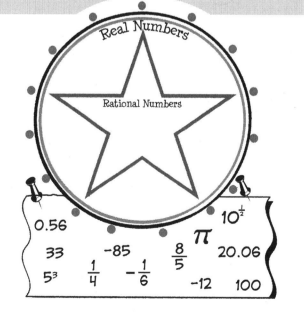

Real Numbers

Rational Numbers

0.56 $10^{\frac{1}{2}}$

33   −85 $\dfrac{8}{5}$ π 20.06

5^3 $\dfrac{1}{4}$ $-\dfrac{1}{6}$ −12   100

1. Is this the correct graph for the statement?

$$x \geq -2$$

2. Circle the number systems to which each one of these belongs.

(R = real, N = natural, W = whole,
IN = integers, RA = rational, IR = irrational)

a) $\frac{7}{8}$ R   N   W   IN   RA   IR

b) **−9**   R   N   W   IN   RA   IR

c) **12**   R   N   W   IN   RA   IR

3. Solve for h: $A = \frac{h}{2}(b + b')$

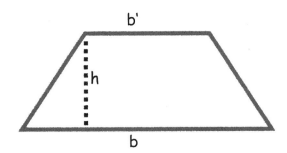

4. Amanda throws all her shoes into a big bag in her closet. There are 15 pairs of shoes—4 pairs are soccer shoes. She reaches in without looking and grabs a shoe. What is the probability that it will be a RIGHT soccer shoe?

5. Challenge Problem

Workers in an athletic shoe warehouse are putting in extra hours today. When the air conditioning went haywire in the huge building, temperatures soared. The glue that held labels onto the shoeboxes dried out and fell off. Now workers had to look inside each box to figure out what style it held. In the first 150 boxes, they found 12 pairs of the $175 *Air Jordan XXII* models.

They used a random sampling method to predict how many of this same style they would find in the total of 2,700 shoeboxes.

Write and solve a proportion to see what they found.

Prediction: They will find _____ pairs of Air Jordan XXII's in 2700 boxes.

Name

1. The expression will reveal the approximate number of pizza restaurants in the United States. Evaluate the expression to find it.

$$60(30^2) + 900\sqrt{81}$$

2. Solve: **3(b + 4b) = 40 – 15 + 20**

3. Finish the sentence:

   Negative six to the sixth power $(-6)^6$ is _____.

4. How many *like terms* are found in this expression?

   $$\frac{1}{2}d + d^2 - 3d^3 + 6d = -7$$

5. Some reports claim that the *Dunkin' Donuts* chain sells 950 million doughnuts in five months. At this rate, how many doughnuts would the chain of shops sell in one year?

Name

1. Which numbers have square roots ≤18?

   $$\sqrt{400} \qquad \sqrt{441} \qquad \sqrt{144}$$
   $$\sqrt{121} \qquad \sqrt{361} \qquad \sqrt{225} \qquad \sqrt{324}$$

2. Colonel Sanders' original white suit (worn in Kentucky Fried Chicken ads) was auctioned off for a hefty sum of money. This amount (in dollars) is a whole number with five even digits. At least one digit is > 5. Four digits are the same, and the sum of the digits is eight. How much was paid for the suit?

3. Write this expression in words:

   $(x^3 – 18) ≥ 25$

4. Solve: $\frac{1}{2} - y = -\frac{1}{2}$

5. One of the world's largest McDonald's restaurants is found in the capital city of China. Its area is 28,000 square feet.

   a. If the length is 400 feet, what is the perimeter?

   b. If the length is 500 feet, what is the perimeter?

LARGE FRIES
758 MG SODIUM

DOUBLE CHEESEBURGER
557 MG SODIUM

GREEN SALAD WITH DRESSING
585 MG SODIUM

1. This number represents the amount (in ounces) of orange juice served in a week (seven days) at Burger King restaurants worldwide: 2.8×10^9.

How many ounces are served in a day? Write the number in standard notation.

2. Is the solution correct?

$$\frac{3}{2}x = -3$$
$$x = -2$$

3. Simplify both sides of the equation:

$$7n - n + n(6) = n^3 + (25 - 8) - 4n^3$$

4. Circle the correct answer:

$$\left(\frac{4}{x}\right)(xy) =$$

$$4y \qquad 4x^2y \qquad 2x \qquad x^2 + 4y$$

5. The signs show the sodium (salt) content in some choices at a fast food restaurant. Peyton ordered (and ate) one of each item shown, taking in 1.9 times the maximum daily recommended amount of sodium. What is the amount recommended for daily consumption?

1. A group of eight friends visited In & Out Burger restaurant and ordered a hamburger with 100 meat patties. It took them two hours to eat the burger, which contained a whopping 19,490 calories.

> If they all ate approximately the same amount at the same speed, how many calories did each person consume in an hour? (Round to the nearest whole number.)

2. Multiply: $-2 \cdot \sqrt{16} \cdot \sqrt{256}$

3. Evaluate for a = 6, b = 4, and c = –3.

$$-2a(b + 2c)$$

4. How many square roots does **–625** have?

5. Which example below is a correct graph of this inequality?

$$2x \geq 3 - 7$$

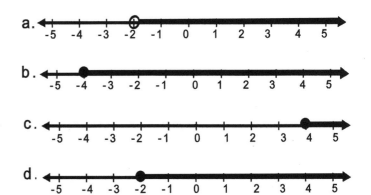

a. (number line from -5 to 5, open circle at -2)

b. (number line from -5 to 5, closed circle at -4, shaded right)

c. (number line from -5 to 5, closed circle at 4)

d. (number line from -5 to 5, closed circle at -2, shaded right)

1. When Burger King opened its doors in 1957, Erik's dad was able to buy a Whopper for 37¢. Yesterday, Erik bought one for $3.33. What is the percent of increase in the price over the years?

2. Explain why $\sqrt{48} = 4\sqrt{3}$.

3. If $xy - 35 - y = -12$, could $y = -7$?

4. Finish the table and write the ordered pairs.

$$3x + y = -4$$

x	y	(x, y)
-5		( )
	2	( )
	-4	( )
	-1	( )
1		( )
3		( )
	-19	( )
6		( )

5. Challenge Problem

Bigbucks Coffee Shop is always trying to make a buck. They blend coffee worth $5.00 a pound with a cheap coffee worth $1.00 a pound to make it taste better. If they want to make 50 pounds of a mixture that costs them $3.00 a pound to make, how much of each grade of coffee would they use?

Use the table to help set up an equation and solve the problem.

Grade	Cost in Cents	# of Pounds	Total Value in Cents
CHEAP	100	X	100X
BETTER	500	50- X	500(50-X)
GRADE	Cost in Cents	# of Pounds	Total Value in Cents
CHEAP	100	X	100X
BETTER	500	50-X	500(50-X)
MIXTURE	300	50	15,000

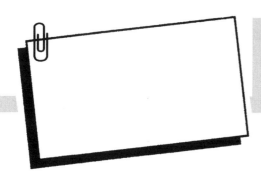

1. A crow flies at a speed of 25 mph. A dragonfly's speed is 18 mph, while some race horses can run at 43 mph. An ostrich runs at a top speed of 45 mph, and an elephant can move up to 25 mph. A cat's top speed is about 6 mph.

   a. What is the median of this group of data?

   b. What is the mode of this group of data?

2. Finish the number sentence to show the commutative property.

   $9x + 33 + x^2 =$ _____

3. The *Apollo 10* spacecraft reentered Earth's atmosphere at a speed of about 18,600 mph. Use scientific notation to write this number.

4. Solve: **$7x - 3 = 5x + 4^2 - 1$**

5. Pedaling at a record-setting speed, a man on a unicycle covered 72 miles in 4 hours.

   a. At this rate, how long would it take him to travel 216 miles?

   b. If, after the first four hours, his rate slowed by 5 mph, how far could he travel in 7 hours?

1. The *Concorde* supersonic jet flew at 1,354 mph. This number is equal to or greater than twice the speed of an ordinary jumbo jet.

   Use j to represent the jumbo jet. Write an expression to show the above information.

2. Evaluate: $\left(\frac{-9}{4}\right)\left(\frac{-6}{27}\right)$

3. Find three different values for **x**.
   $x \le \sqrt{121}$

4. Solve: **$3b^2 + 10 = 110 - b^2$**

5. A submarine and a penguin have something in common: They can both move swiftly through water. Combined, their speeds total 74 mph. The sub's speed is 8 mph greater than twice the penguin's speed.

   Write and solve an equation to find the speeds of these two "swimmers."

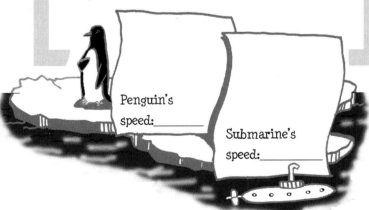

Penguin's speed: _____

Submarine's speed: _____

20

1. Which operation is done last?

$15 + (6)(3)(12 - 9)^2$

2. Japan's bullet train travels at 143 mph. This is 8.7% of the speed of a real bullet shot from a rifle. What is the approximate speed of the rifle bullet?

3. Simplify:

$6 + 3x - 4 + x \geq y + 9 - 3y + 5$

4. Find and describe the error that was made in the process of solving this equation.

$4p + 3 + 2p = 3 - 6$

$6p + 3 = -3$

$6p = 0$

$p = 0$

5. Write T (true) or F (false) for each statement.

___a. To add two exponential numbers with different coefficients, add the coefficients, then add the exponents.

___b. You cannot add exponential numbers with different bases.

___c. To subtract two exponential numbers with the same coefficient, subtract the bases and keep the coefficient the same.

___d. You cannot subtract any exponential number from another exponential number.

1. Multiply: $(\sqrt[4]{16})(\sqrt{0})$

2. Evaluate for **x = –6**.

$$\frac{8x - 28}{2x^2 + 4}$$

3. The fastest sneeze recorded traveled at one hundred three and six-tenths miles per hour. Use standard notation to write a number that is twelve and nine hundredths less than that number.

4. Factor: $3ab^2 + 9a - 12a$

5. Circle any statements about a linear equation that are TRUE.

a. It has more than two variables.

b. IT CONTAINS NO VARIABLE WITH POWERS > 1.

c. There is no variable in the denominator of any fraction.

d. Its graph can be a straight or curved line.

e. It may involve one or more basic operations (addition, subtraction, multiplication, division).

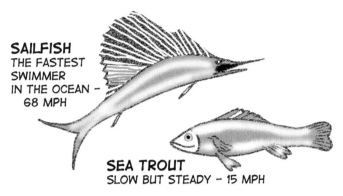

SAILFISH
THE FASTEST
SWIMMER
IN THE OCEAN –
68 MPH

SEA TROUT
SLOW BUT STEADY – 15 MPH

1. Write two different expressions to show the relationship between the speed of the sailfish and the speed of the sea trout. Use **s** to represent the sailfish speed and **t** to represent the trout speed.

2. Solve:

$$5(2n - 2) = 3(n - 1) + 7$$

3. Seven spiders and five turtles are racing. All are moving at a similar pace of 0.25 mph. What is the probability that the winner could be a spider?

$\dfrac{5}{7}$ $\qquad$ $\dfrac{7}{12}$ $\qquad$ $\dfrac{5}{12}$ $\qquad$ $\dfrac{7}{5}$

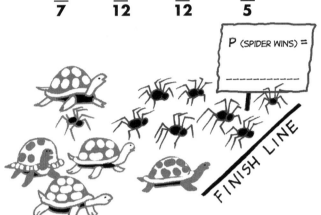

P (SPIDER WINS) =
_____

FINISH LINE

4. Multiply:

$$(9x + x^2)(y + 5)$$

5. Challenge Problem

Two trains travel on tracks that run parallel to each other. Their starting points are 3740 miles apart. The first train, the *Silver Streak*, travels from northwest to southeast at 90 mph. The second train, the *Red Blaze*, travels from southeast to northwest at 80 mph. They start their journeys at the same time—midnight EST—and move toward each other. Assume that they travel at steady speeds without stops and without interruption.

a. At what time will the trains meet?

b. How far will the *Silver Streak* have traveled when they meet?

c. How far will the *Red Blaze* have traveled when they meet?

d. Explain how you solved the problem.

1. When the electronics store at the mall opened on Monday morning, 39 of the hot new video game system models were on the shelf. By noon, they had sold all of those and taken money for orders of 429 more. Write a number to show the ratio of the total number sold to the number originally on the shelf.

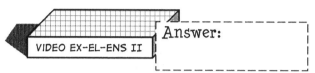

VIDEO EX-EL-ENS II

Answer: _____

2. Write this expression in words: $\sqrt[3]{x} = 15$

3. Simplify: $6x^0 =$

4. Solve: $-c + 8 + 6c = c - 40$

5. The largest mall in the world is the West Edmonton Mall in Alberta, Canada. It even holds an amusement park. This park, Galaxyland, covers an area of 4×10^5 square feet. The mall's area is 5.3×10^6 square feet.

Use standard notation to write a number showing the difference in the two areas.

1. Simplify:
$15x^2 - 10x + 13 + 12x - 8$

2. What is the value of $\sqrt[3]{216}$?

3. Evaluate: $-12 - (-6) + 20 - 4^2 =$

4. Kendra started the day with $186.00 in her checking account. She wrote five checks at the mall, but forgot to record one. Five days later, the other four checks had cleared and her bank balance was $35.30. The other checks were: $18.00, $25.75, $30.00, and $12.00. Write and solve an equation to find the amount of the missing check.

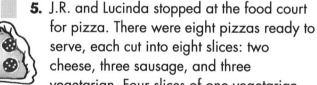

5. J.R. and Lucinda stopped at the food court for pizza. There were eight pizzas ready to serve, each cut into eight slices: two cheese, three sausage, and three vegetarian. Four slices of one vegetarian pizza had been served, but the others were complete pizzas.

a. Lucinda told the server to give her one slice of any pizza. What is the probability that she would get a slice of sausage pizza?

b. J.R. gave the same instruction to the server. If Lucinda got sausage, what is the probability that he would also?

1. Choose the expressions written as sentences.

   ○ $-10 \geq x$ ○ $-6m + 9m$ ○ $3x \approx 4y$

   ○ $12 - 3 \cdot c$ ○ $77 < y$ ○ $(4p)(7p)$

2. Simplify: $4n^8 + (3n^2)(2n^6)$

3. A group of friends met at the mall and stayed 4 hours and 15 minutes. They spent 1 hour and 20 minutes in the music store, 55 minutes in the food court, 75 minutes in the sports store, and $\frac{3}{4}$ hour wandering. They left at 5:10 p.m. What time did they arrive?

TIME ARRIVED:

TIME DEPARTED:

5:10 PM

4. Evaluate:

$$5^4 - \sqrt[3]{-8}$$

5. The West Edmonton Mall has the world's largest parking lot. It holds 20,000 vehicles at one time and has an overflow lot that holds another 10,000. Assume that the average vehicle is 16 ft long and 5 ft wide. Assume also that a two-foot space is needed between vehicles for safe parking.

Could the total area of these parking lots be less than 3.5 million square feet?

1. Factor: $4xy - 12y + 16y^2$

2. Does x have a real number solution?

    $x = \sqrt{-25}$

3. Which of these expressions have a value that is ≥ 30 for $z = 7$ and $w = 3$?

   ○ $z(2 + w)$ ○ $\frac{6z}{w}$

   ○ $3(z + 4 - w)$ ○ $w(w + z)$

4. Graph the inequality:

    $3 + x \geq -1$

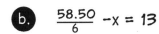

5. Which equation can be used to solve the problem below?

Lindsay bought six CDs at the mall. The original price was $13 each, but she got a discount, and only paid a total of $58.50 for all six. What was the discount?

    a. $(13)(6x) = 58.50$

    b. $\frac{58.50}{6} - x = 13$

    c. $6(13 - 13x) = 58.50$

    d $6x + 58.50 = 13$

    e. $13 + \frac{x}{58.50} = 6$

1. Complete the table. Then graph the equation.

x – y = 0		
x	y	(x, y)
–2		
–1		
1		
2		

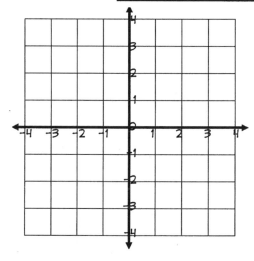

2. Terryl shopped for some workout clothes. He narrowed his selections down to three shirts (red, white, black), four pairs of pants (gray, red, white, black), and two pairs of shoes (yellow, blue). He can buy only one of each. How many different combinations of shirts, pants, and shoes are possible?

3. Evaluate:

a. $|6| =$ c. $6\,|-6| =$

b. $|-6| =$ d. $\dfrac{|-6|}{6} =$

4. If negative two times a number is the sum of the number and eighty-four, what is the number?

5. Challenge Problem

Jayde goes to the mall with a sum of money and spends it all. She spends . . .

- one-third of the money on clothes
- six dollars on a fake tattoo
- one-half the amount on food that she spent on clothes

- twenty percent of the money on CDs
- three-twelfths of the money on books

How much money did she bring with her to the mall?

_____

Show how you arrived at the solution.

1. In ten shows, a magician pulled rabbits from a hat. The numbers pulled in those ten shows were: **15, 4, 9, 16, 12, 9, 12, 16, 3, 11**.

   How many modes can be found in this set of data?

2. Solve: **4n + 5 = 15**

3. Use the *powers of a power property* to simplify the expression:

   $$(10^4)^2 =$$

4. One of Harry Houdini's famous tricks involved the disappearance of a large elephant. To find a number equal to the weight of that elephant (in pounds), give the value of the expression:

   $$-100^2$$

5. There are claims that David Copperfield is the world's highest-earning magician and illusionist. His 2005 proceeds from shows and endorsements totaled $57 million.

   If he earned $32 million from endorsements and $5 million per show, how many shows did he perform in 2005?

ANSWER:

1. A donor offered a dollar amount for each second that an escape artist could stay underwater in a large glass container. The amount totaled seventy-eight dollars after thirteen seconds. At this rate, how much would the donor pay for a full two minutes?

2. Solve: $\sqrt{x + 2} = 5$

3. Use numbers and symbols to write the statement:

   The difference between two times a number and five squared is greater than twelve.

4. Solve: **p – 12 = 3p + 4**

5. Complete the magic square using the numbers 1 through 16, each one time. All rows (horizontal, vertical, and diagonal) add up to the sum of 34.

		5	8
	14		
	7	9	
	2		

1. Simplify the product:

$$(10x^4y)(3x^2y^4)$$

2.

FIND THE UNKNOWN NUMBERS

Three consecutive even integers add up to 42.

What are the integers?

3. Simplify: $\dfrac{6ab^2}{-2ab}$

4. Is the equation solved correctly?

$$\frac{x}{2} - 4\frac{1}{3} = 2\frac{1}{4}$$

$$x = 4\frac{1}{6}$$

5. David Blaine, famous street magician, stood in a closet of ice in Times Square for 61 hours and 40 minutes. At another time, he stood on a pillar for a different length of time. The total time for the two feats is $6\frac{1}{2}$ hours less than 102 hours and 33 minutes. How long did David stand on the pillar?

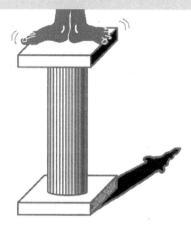

1. Simplify: $(2\sqrt{5})^2$

2. Evaluate for **n = –5** and **p = –9**.

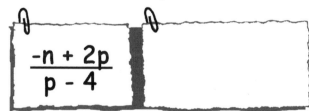

$$\frac{-n + 2p}{p - 4}$$

3. Solve: $\dfrac{x}{2} + 6 = \dfrac{2x}{5} + 7$

4. An escape artist is secured in a chest wrapped in chains. The chest hangs from a crane and is 16 feet above the waterline. Then it is lowered to the sea bottom, 68 feet below the surface. Write and solve a subtraction sentence to find the difference between the starting location and the resting spot of the chest.

5. Circle statements that are true.

$$5^2 - 33 \geq 23$$

$$(\sqrt{64})(\sqrt{121}) \neq \frac{440}{5}$$

$$4\sqrt[3]{125} > 3\sqrt[3]{64}$$

$$\frac{1}{5}x = \frac{3}{15}x$$

Name

1. 5,320 is eighty percent of what number?

2. Use the Pythagorean theorem to find the length of the missing side.

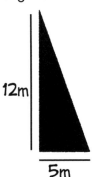

12m

5m

3. A magician found that her injuries increased after she started doing tricks with knives and fire. After doing 15 shows, she had a total of 735 cuts, nicks, bruises, and burns. At this rate, how many shows did she do to accumulate 294 such injuries?

4. Put these numbers in order from smallest to largest.

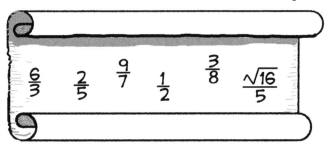

$$\frac{6}{3} \quad \frac{2}{5} \quad \frac{9}{7} \quad \frac{1}{2} \quad \frac{3}{8} \quad \frac{\sqrt{16}}{5}$$

5. Challenge Problem

At a magic show, the magician holds these cards in his hands.
A member of the audience draws a card without looking.

   a. What is the probability it will be a club?

   b. What is the probability it will NOT be an even number or a club? *(Assume ace value = 1)*

   c. What is the probability it will NOT be a number > 4? *(Assume ace value = 1)*

   d. The participant draws two cards from this group of cards. What is the probability she will draw a 4 of spades followed by the ace of clubs?

1. The hula hoop was one of the hottest fads in the U.S. during the 1950s. This fun new toy sold as fast as 20,000 a day for a while. This number can be written as

   ○ $(\sqrt{10,000})\ (2 \times 10^3)$

   ○ $5(40^3)$

   ○ $2(10^4)\ (1^2)$

2. Write **6,240,000,000** in scientific notation.

3. Which of these—4, 5, 6, 7, or 8—is the solution to the number sentence below?

   $(9 \cdot x) + 12 = (12 \cdot x) - 6$

4. Solve:

   $$-8w = -80$$

5. In 1957, the Wham-O Company sold 25 million hula hoops in two months. Assume that each of those two months had 31 days, and use **h** to represent an hour. Which equation(s) can be used to find the number of hula hoops sold in an hour?

   a. $\dfrac{4 \cdot 7 \cdot 24}{25,000,000} = h$

   b. $h(2 \cdot 31 \cdot 24) = 25,000,000$

   c. $1488h = 25,000,000$

   d. $25,000,000h = 2 \cdot 24 \cdot 31$

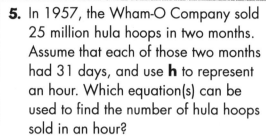

1. Write a number sentence to show the Identity Property for Multiplication.

2. One of the most interesting fads of the 1920s was flagpole sitting. A record-holder sat on top of a flagpole for 49 days. In minutes, this is closest to

   a. $(30^3)\ (2^4)$ min   **c. 42^3 min**

   b. $(16^4) + (8^4)$ min   **d. $(25^3)\ (-2^2)$**

3. Write the expression in words:

   $(-7 + 3)\sqrt[3]{343}$

4. Which is the value of x in the equation below: **12, $\frac{1}{2}$, 4,** or **3**?

   $$\left(\frac{6}{x}\right)\left(\frac{1}{2}\right) = \frac{3}{4}$$

5. A fad involving the use of a simple word grew fast in the 1980's. It is still quite popular today. People "negate" an idea by saying it, then adding the word . . .

If you drew one letter of the alphabet at random...

   a. What is the probability of drawing a letter in the word?

   b. What is the probability of drawing a letter not in the word?

   c. With three consecutive drawings, what is the probability of drawing all three letters in the word?

1. Is the solution correct?

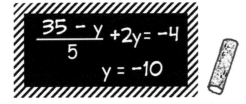

$$\frac{35 - y}{5} + 2y = -4$$
$$y = -10$$

2. Simplify: $3x^5 + 6x^5 + (-12x^5)$

3. Getting tattooed is a fad that has lasted for centuries. Lucky Rich of Australia is one of the most tattooed persons in the world. He has tattoos on 99.9% of the surface of his skin. The average adult human body has about 2 square meters of skin covering. About how much surface on Lucky's body is not covered with tattoos?

4. Identify the *like* terms in this expression.
$$4b^2 + 3c - 6c - 6b - 2b^2$$

5. One of the hottest fads of the 1950s was telephone booth stuffing. The challenge in this activity was to see how many people could fit into a phone booth at one time. Write an equation and use it to solve the problem below.

One group that got stuffed into a phone booth included 18 adults and 9 children. Each child took up $\frac{2}{3}$ the space of an adult. The phone booth was 2.8 feet wide and 2.8 feet deep with a height of 6.9 feet. Approximately how much space was occupied by each adult?

1. Simplify: $\sqrt[6]{64}$

2. The popularity of the Slinky toy (a 1940s fad) has lasted for decades. It is an 87-foot length of wire wrapped in 3-inch diameter circular coils.

   Is there enough information given above to estimate the number of coils in a Slinky?

3. Simplify: $5(n - 3) - 3(2 + n) - (n + 7)$

4. Write the reciprocal of each:

   $$-8 \quad 3X \quad X-2$$
   $$\frac{5}{4} \quad \frac{-X}{5} \quad 3\frac{1}{3}$$

Beanie Babies
Beanie Babies became wildly popular in the 1990s. The craze was fueled when MacDonald's restaurants included one of the toys in every Happy Meal. When the restaurant chain started this practice, 100 million were sold in a matter of a few days. The average number of sales for each of those days was 7,142,857.

5. Which equation will find the number of days to reach sales of 100 million?

   a. $7,142,857x = 100,000,000$

   b. $100,000,000x = 7,142,857$

   c. $\frac{x}{100,000,000} = 7,142,857$

1. Drive-in movies were popular in the 1930s and 1940s. In 1933, there were 100 drive-in theaters in the U.S. By 1945, there were 2,200. What was the percent of increase from 1933 to 1945?

2. Which operation should be done *last*?

$$(12 - 7)4 + 5^3 - 16 + 3(10 + 3)$$

3. Which has the least value?
*(In all expressions, **d = 100** and **c = 10**.)*

$$c(d + c) \qquad \frac{10c}{d} \qquad \frac{d}{10(5c)}$$

4. Graph the solution.

$$2 - x > -3$$

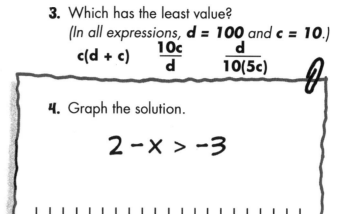

5. Challenge Problem

The "Flying Saucer" toy, as it was first known, was a huge fad in the 1950s. It was renamed Frisbee and has sold over 200 million in the past 50 years. Use the formula **rt = d** *(rate times time equals distance)* or one of its variations to solve the following problems about the flying toy.

a. Zack threw his Frisbee. It traveled 70 feet in 44 seconds. What is the rate in feet per second?

b. Zola's Frisbee traveled a distance of 143 feet at a rate of 2.2 feet per second. How long did this take?

c. One toss by Zelda sent a Frisbee flying for 110 seconds at 1.6 feet per second. Zeke tossed his Frisbee at the same time. It traveled 2.5 feet per second for 85 seconds. What is the difference in the distance covered by the two Frisbees?

d. Z. Z.'s Frisbee flew at a rate of 3 feet per second for a distance of 58.5 feet. How much time did it fly?

e. Mom, competing with her four kids, threw a fantastic toss. Her Frisbee flew 609 feet. It was airborne for 145 seconds. What was the rate of travel?

f. A crate of Frisbees traveled on a plane flying from Boston to Miami. The plane left the ground at 11:52 a.m. and landed (in the same time zone) at 3:04 p.m. The plane traveled at a rate of 393 miles per hour. What is the distance between Boston and Miami (rounded to the nearest mile)?

1. In an unusual display of human endurance, Eufermina Stadler ironed for 40 hours without stopping. In that time, she ironed 228 sheets. At that rate, how long did it take her to iron 171 sheets?

2. How many variables are found in this expression?

$$n - 2n^2 + 5n^3 + 7n$$

3. Simplify: $7\sqrt{27} - 3\sqrt{12}$

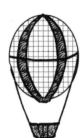

4. Circle the irrational numbers below.

$$\sqrt{7} \qquad \sqrt[3]{8} \qquad \mathbf{52} \qquad \sqrt{10} \qquad \frac{1}{160} \qquad 4.101$$

5. Mike Howard of the United Kingdom can be proud of his amazing achievement. He walked on a beam suspended between two hot air balloons at an altitude of 21,400 feet.

What is the approximate altitude in meters?

Answer:

1. Evaluate for $x = -2$

$$(x + 1)(x + 2)(x - 3)$$

2. In a most unusual human feat, Garry Turner clipped a record-breaking number of clothespins to his face at one time. To find the number, simplify:

$$\sqrt[3]{216} + 3^5 - (2 \cdot 3^2 \cdot 5)$$

3. Circle the correct solution for the following number sentence.

28   –28   –22   22   75   –75

$$-25 - (-3) + 16 - 16 =$$

4. Use words to write this equation:

$$35 = p + (-2q)$$

5. Represent sets A and B in the Venn diagram.

$$A = \{-6, \tfrac{2}{3}, 6.75, -30, \sqrt[3]{-64}, \tfrac{1}{2}, 8, 42\}$$

$$B = \{-8, -\tfrac{1}{2}, \tfrac{1}{2}, 5.44, -3, 42, 6.75\}$$

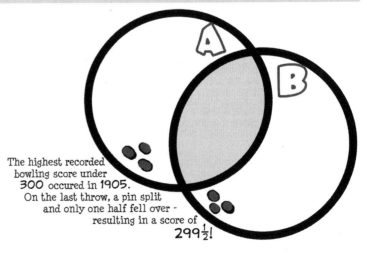

The highest recorded bowling score under 300 occured in 1905. On the last throw, a pin split and only one half fell over – resulting in a score of $299\tfrac{1}{2}$!

1. Simplify:

$$3y(15 + 5) - 2y(3 - 2) + \frac{12y + 6}{3}$$

2. In an astounding show of strength, Thomas Blackthorne lifted 24 lb, 3 oz of weight with his tongue. In kilograms, this weight is closest to:

48 kg   96 kg   9 kg   11 kg   109 kg

3. Multiply: $(2w^2)(3w^6)$

4. Which solution has a greater value if **p** is a negative number?

a.
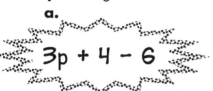
$3p + 4 - 6$

b.
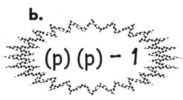
$(p)(p) - 1$

5. Write and solve an equation to answer the question.

A record-setting journey on a tractor covered 3,425 miles from June 12 to July 5, 2004. Assuming the driver traveled 12 hours a day and rested five of the days, what was the rate of travel (miles per hour rounded to the nearest tenth)?

1. Write the prime factors of twenty-eight.

2. Simplify and solve:

$$\frac{1}{2} \times \geq 3$$

3. What is **x** in the equation below?

$$\sqrt[x]{125} = 5$$

4. Drummer Oliver Butterworth set a record for the most drumbeats per minute: one thousand eighty. Four-fifths of this number is seventeen less than half of another number of drum beats (b).

5. A group of school children in the UK laid down a row of 79,200 pennies in 2 hours, 42 minutes, and 29 seconds. At that rate, about how many pennies did they lay down in 1 hour and 40 minutes?

Choose the closest answer.

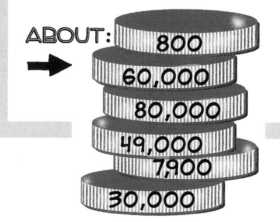

ABOUT: 800
60,000
80,000
49,000
7,900
30,000

1. A man from Italy holds the record for smashing 22 watermelons with his head in one minute. If the volume of one of the spherical watermelons is 232 inches^3, is it likely that the melon has a 6-inch radius?

2. Finish the sentence to show the distributive property:

   $6x(x^2 + y - 3z) =$

3. Here are three of the final amounts of weight lifted by one competitor in four contests: 200.7 kg, 198.5 kg, and 236 kg. The total for the four contests was 835.2 kg. What is the mean of the four scores?

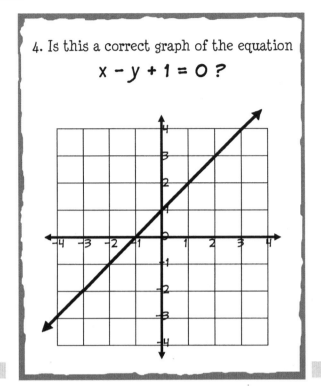

4. Is this a correct graph of the equation
$$x - y + 1 = 0 \, ?$$

5. Challenge Problem

Each barbell should hold two numbers that have the same value. Find each missing number among the numbers below and write it on the correct barbell.

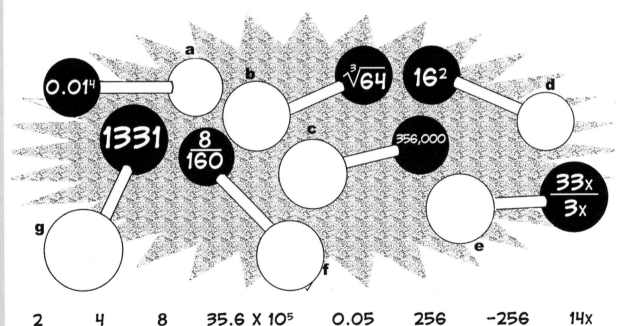

2	4	8	35.6 X 10^5	0.05	256	−256	14x
	0.00001		3.56 X 10^5	11x	3x^2 + 11	0.2	
11^3	$\frac{1}{2}$	0.00000001		3.46 X 10^6	11		

1. Detective Sandra Sly went shopping for some new disguises and paid $182.52 for a wig, clothes, glasses, and makeup. This included 8% tax. What was the bill without the tax?

2. Simplify: $(4x)(10y)(\frac{1}{4}X)$

3. Which example shows the associative property?

   a. $(3.5 + 6.7)x = 3.5x + 6.7x$
   b. $(xy)^2 (1) = x^2y^2$
   c. $a(b^2c^2) = (ab^2)c^2$

4. Evaluate each expression.

   X^{-5} 6^{-3} $\dfrac{3^{-2}}{4}$

5. Use the information and the diagram to decide which suspect could have been the shadowy figure.

Just after a jewelry store theft, a witness saw a shadowy figure hiding against a building nearby. She noticed that the shadow of the figure reached just to the edge of the sidewalk. Investigators measured to find the distances. Four suspects were apprehended. Their heights were:
Lou: 6 ft, 9 in;
Axel: 4 ft, 10 in;
Maxi: 5 ft, 7 in;
and Sue: 6 ft.

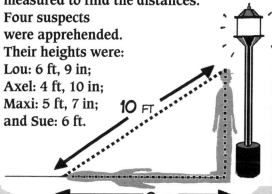

10 FT

8 FT

1. Solve: $66 = 2 + \dfrac{x}{5}$

2. Use numbers and symbols to write the following expression:

   The length of the movie *The Pink Panther* (m) is greater than seventy-five minutes and less than ninety-nine minutes.

3. Evaluate: $\sqrt[5]{243}$

4.
   A thief used a skateboard as a getaway vehicle. The robbery was at 10:15 PM. She has been moving ever since at 6.5 mph, and is 26 miles from the scene. What time is it?

5. A great detective movie, *The Pink Panther* (2006), took in a large amount of money at the box office. Use the clues to find the dollar amount.

CLUES:

- THE NUMBER HAS FOUR PRIME FACTORS.

- TWO OF THE PRIME FACTORS ARE 733 AND 5099.

- THE OTHER TWO FACTORS HAVE A PRODUCT OF 22.

1. A private investigator watched a suspect for a total of 32.5 hours for three days. On Tuesday, he watched 8 hours more than half as many as on Monday. On Wednesday, he watched twice the hours as on Monday. How many hours did he watch on Tuesday?

2. Simplify both sides of the equation.

$$\frac{2}{3}x + 6x - 7 + 2 = \sqrt{10,000} - 5^2$$

3. Agatha Christie's mystery, *The Mousetrap*, is the longest running play in London. To find the number of performances as of 2006, simplify the expression.

$$2^3 \cdot 2^2 \cdot 5^2 \cdot 5^2$$

4. Circle the simplification for **(4x) (6x)**.

$10x$	$24x$	$24x^2$
$10x^2$	$2x^2$	$2x$

5.

5. A thief is trying to transport some cash, all in the demonination of $50 bills. The money is bundled in stacks of 150 bills each, measuring 2 inches thick. A bill is 2.5 inches wide and 9 inches long. Could the thief fit $75,000 in this briefcase?

1. The oldest bank robber on record was arrested by a detective who was much younger. The sum of their ages was 133 years, and the difference was 51 years. What was the age of the robber?

2. Evaluate: $-100y + \sqrt{10,000y^2}$

3. The mystery novels of Agatha Christie, "the Queen of Crime," have sold forty million copies in France alone. Is this the same number as $2,000^2$?

4. Simplify for **x > 0**.

$$\sqrt{(81x)^2}$$

5. Private Investigator Samuel I. Snoop solved 42 cold cases in 12 weeks. At this rate . . .

   a. how long will it take him to solve 77 cases?

   b. did he solve at least 17 cases in five weeks?

   c. how many cases could he solve in 15 weeks?

THESE ARE REALLY COLD CASES!

1. Evaluate:

Negative fifty-eight divided by half of negative eight equals

2. Which is the correct graph of **2 x − 2 < x + 3**?

a.

b.

3. Solve: $\frac{1}{4n} + 20 > 12$

4. Detective Dewey Surch investigated 170 burglaries in the past six months This is 85% of all the cases he handled in that time. What was the detective's case load?

230   370

250   200

144

310

5. Challenge Problem

A group of sharp detectives confiscated several bags of stolen money. Follow the clues on the outside of each bag to find out what's inside.

A. $7,100
- TOTAL OF 177 BILLS
- THREE KINDS OF U.S. BILLS: 5'S, 50'S, & 100'S
WHAT ARE THE BILLS?

B. $68.50
- 440 U.S. COINS
- THREE KINDS OF COINS
WHAT ARE THE COINS?

C. 300 U.S. Bills
- THREE DIFFERENT KINDS OF BILLS
WHAT IS THE GREATEST AMOUNT THAT COULD BE IN THE BAG?
WHAT IS THE LEAST AMOUNT THAT COULD BE IN THE BAG?

D.
HOW MUCH IS LEFT IN THE BAG?
A ROBBER LEFT THE BANK WITH $14,000 IN BILLS. DUE TO A HOLE IN THE BAG, ONE-FIFTH WAS LEFT. LATER, TWO-SEVENTHS OF THE REMAINING AMOUNT FELL OUT THROUGH THE HOLE.

E.
HOW MUCH IS IN THE BAG?
- CONTAINS 48% OF TOTAL AMOUNT IN BANK VAULT
- $214,240 IS LEFT IN THE BANK VAULT

F.
HOW MUCH IS IN THE BAG?
- 5 EVEN DIGITS, ALL > 0
- FOUR ARE THE SAME
- GREATEST DIGIT IN TENS PLACE
- SUM OF DIGITS EQUALS 14

1. The coldest place in the Milky Way galaxy is found in the Boomerang Nebula. The temperature is $-457.6°$ F.Convert this to a Celsius temperature. *(Use the formula F = $\frac{9}{5}$C + 32)*

2. Write this expression in words:

$$17 \geq x^2 - (-1)$$

3. The world's fastest-moving glacier travels 115 feet a day. Another glacier is one mile away. It moves 80 feet a day toward the first glacier. In approximately how many days will they meet? *(1 mi = 5,280 ft)*

4. Evaluate:

$$X^{-3} = \boxed{} \blacktriangleright$$

5. Which are not linear equations?

a. $-\frac{3}{5}t = 226$

b. $7b - 2(a + b) = 7$

c. $n^2 + y = 15$

d. $x = 7 + 3$

e. $p + q = -19$

f. $(x + y)^3 - 2x = 25$

-128°F   **coldest recorded temperature**

136.4°F   **warmest recorded temperature**

1. Write a subtraction sentence to find the difference between the two temperatures.

2. Fill in the blank with **<**, **>**, or **=**.

$$\sqrt[3]{512} \underline{} \sqrt{49}$$

3. Write this expression in words: $\frac{c^2}{cd}$

4. The solution is **x = -6**. Choose the problem.

○ $3x - 9 + x = 2x$

○ $x^2 + 7x = 6$

○ $4x = 2x + 12$

5. Find the difference between the volumes of the two ice blocks.

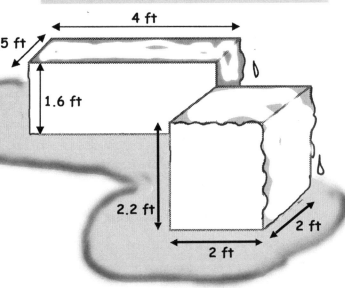

4 ft

1.5 ft

1.6 ft

2.2 ft

2 ft

2 ft

1. In a wild hailstorm, the icy hailstones are accumulating at a rate of 1500 per second. There are now 50,000 on the ground. At the same rate, how much longer will it take to accumulate a total of 200,000?

2. Simplify:

$$\frac{n^{10}}{n^3}$$

3. A sequence begins **4, 16, 28, 40, 52, 64, 76 . . .** Each term after that follows the same pattern shown here. Which term will be **280**?

4. Is the expression simplified correctly?
   $$x - [6 + 2(8 - 1)] = x + 20$$

5. Assume the spinner below will be spun once. Find the probabilities for the results described.

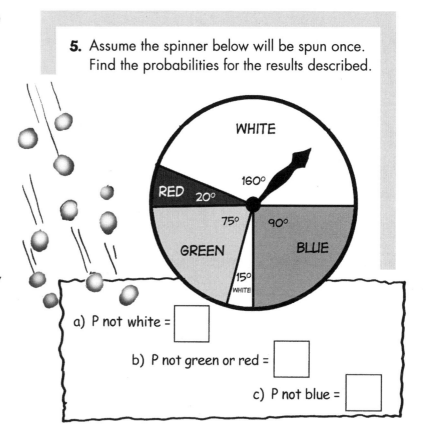

a) P not white = ☐

b) P not green or red = ☐

c) P not blue = ☐

1. Circle the choices that accurately complete the sentence:

   Thirty-seven is a(n)_____ number.

   natural   counting   whole

         real   negative

   integer   irrational   rational

2. Simplify: $\sqrt{(4)(9)}$

3. Graph: $\frac{1}{2}x \geq 3$

   -10 -9 -8 -7 -6 -5 -4 -3 -2 -1 0 1 2 3 4 5 6 7 8 9 10

4. A patch of ice **x** feet long melts **y** feet from one end and 7 feet from the other end.

   Write two different expressions to show the remaining length of the ice patch.

Ice Cube Toss Results

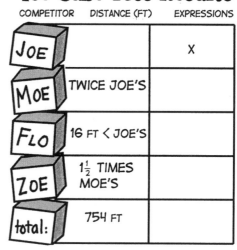

COMPETITOR	DISTANCE (FT)	EXPRESSIONS
JOE		X
MOE	TWICE JOE'S	
FLO	16 FT < JOE'S	
ZOE	$1\frac{1}{2}$ TIMES MOE'S	
total:	754 FT	

5. Fill in all the blanks on the table to show the appropriate expressions and the correct distance for Joe's toss.

1. The following ice sculptures won the top five places in an ice sculpture competition: a mermaid, an Eiffel Tower, an ice skate, a pair of swans, and a Volkswagen Beetle. How many different placing results (permutations) are possible (for first, second, third, fourth, fifth places)?

2. Evaluate: $\dfrac{-66}{2(-11)}$

3. Solve for y: $3y + 5 > 7$

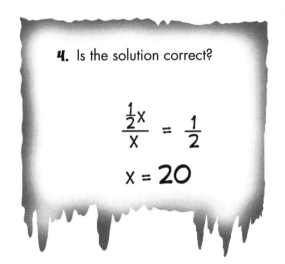

4. Is the solution correct?

$$\dfrac{\frac{1}{2}x}{x} = \dfrac{1}{2}$$

$$x = 20$$

5. Challenge Problem

Find the equation to match each graph. Write the equation above the graph.

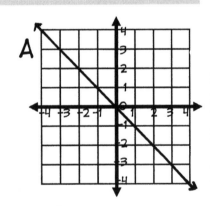

A

$x + y = 2$
$x^2 = y$
$y = 2x + 1$
$x + y = -1$
$x = -y$
$y = x + 2$
$x - 3 = y$
$y = -x + 3$

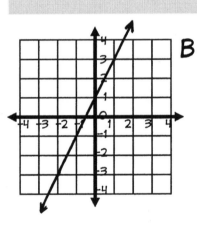

B

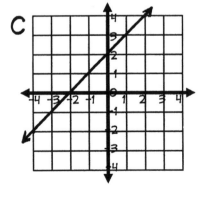

C

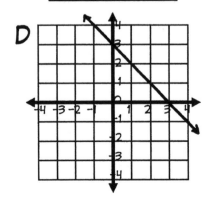

D

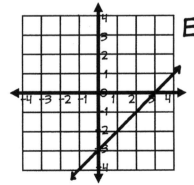

E

Name

1. The United States has the world's highest consumption of soda pop. The average person drinks 87.2 gallons of soda a year. About how many 12-ounce cans of soda is this?

SPECIAL!
6-PACK OF
Onion Soda

2. Evaluate: $-4(-2)^2$

3. Circle examples that are not equations.

   a) 2 + 10 + 4 = 16   d) 0 = 29 • 0

   b) 8 n = –4   e) x + y < 40

   c) 16 y > 5x   f) 8n – 4

4. Solve: $-\frac{1}{3}x + 22 = 2x - 3$

---

5. Brian Duffield holds the record for being the world's fastest raw onion eater. He ate a 7.47-ounce onion in 1 minute, 32 seconds.

   a. What is the rate at which he ate this onion (in ounces per second)? *Round to the nearest hundredth.*

   b If he could continue at this rate, how long would it take him to eat a 10-oz onion?

   c. If he could continue at this rate, how many 6-ounce onions could he eat in $7\frac{1}{2}$ minutes?

Name

1. It took Mat Hand three minutes to eat 133 grapes. This set a world record for fast grape-eating. At that rate, could he eat 1,000 grapes in 20 minutes?

2. Which expression has greater value?

$\sqrt[3]{17{,}576}$ $\sqrt[5]{59{,}049}$

3. Write this in numbers and symbols:

   The cube root of two hundred sixteen is greater than or equal to the sum of a number (x) and the square root of nine.

4. Give two possible values for **x** in the equation below.

   $x^2 + 2x = 24$

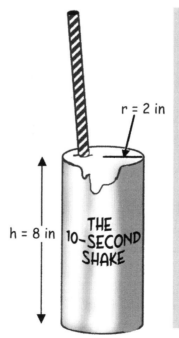

r = 2 in

h = 8 in

THE
10-SECOND
SHAKE

5. The world's fastest milkshake drinker consumed a 500-ml shake in ten seconds. Did he drink more or less than the amount that could fit in this glass? *(Assume the glass holds 34 ml per 10 cubic inches of space.)*

1. Residents in the United Kingdom are the top eaters of breakfast! The average person eats 171 lb, 10 oz of breakfast each year. Convert this measurement to grams.

2. Simplify: $-4x(2x^3)$

3. In which equation is **x** not equal to **10**?

   a) $\frac{9x^2}{10} - 5 = 7x + 15$

   b) $3(x + 7) - 12 = 5x - 11$

   c) $x^2 - 8x + 3x - 24 = 126$

4. Simplify both sides of the equation.
   $5(2n - 2) = 3(n - 1) + 7$

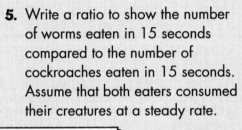

World Record
Fastest Worm Eating

200 Worms in
30 Seconds

C. Manoharan Manu,
India

5. Write a ratio to show the number of worms eaten in 15 seconds compared to the number of cockroaches eaten in 15 seconds. Assume that both eaters consumed their creatures at a steady rate.

World Record
Fastest Cockroach Eating

36 Cockroaches
in **One** Minute

Ken Edwards, UK

1. In 2003, residents of Finland each drank on the average of 1,682 cups of coffee in the year. People in Ireland drank the most tea: 1,302 cups each, on average.

   Assume that each cup held **8 ounces**. Find the difference (per person, in ounces) between the amounts consumed.

2. Simplify: $\sqrt{25x^2} + \sqrt[4]{16x^4}$

3. Evaluate each expression for **y = –6**.

   a) **7y**   b) $\frac{y}{72}$ c) $y^2 - 10y$

4.
> Explain how you determine the slope of a line from looking at its graph.

5. It took Zaphod Xerxes only 4 min, 56 sec to eat a 12-inch pizza. This set a record for the fastest time to eat this size pizza.

   Assuming he ate at a steady rate, how long would it take him to eat a slice of this pizza that had an outside edge with a measurement of 6.28 inches?

YUM!

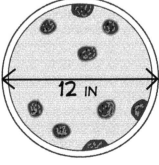

12 IN

Name

1. Fill in the missing numbers on the table.

FRACTION	DECIMAL	PERCENT
$\frac{7}{8}$		
		36%
	0.2	
		12%
	0.8	
$1\frac{3}{10}$	1.3	130%

2. Explain how you can tell if this is a linear equation.

$$12x(5 + 2x) - 6x^2 = 50x^2 - 8$$

3. Solve: *(Remember that there are two cases for absolute value.)*

$$|3x - 2| = 10$$

4. Graph the inequality: $2x \leq -1$

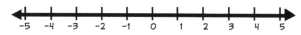

-5 -4 -3 -2 -1 0 1 2 3 4 5

Show your work here:

5. Challenge Problem

At an eating competition, two competitors (John "Hog" Hanner and Benjamin Belch) vied for the championship cookie-eating trophy. John ate twenty cookies an hour more than Ben. In the time it took for all the cookies in the monstrous cookie jar to be eaten, John ate 210 cookies, while Ben ate 90.

a. How many cookies did each competitor eat per hour?

b. What was the total time to eat all the cookies?

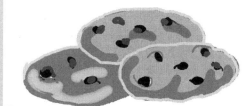

Name

1. A blue whale is the largest animal on Earth. This creature can grow to five feet more than three times the length of a reticulated python. Together, their lengths equal 145 ft. How long is the whale?

2. Evaluate: $6(3)^{-3}$

3. The largest finger painting on record has an area of 5,100 ft². Which of these could be its dimensions?

    a. 189 ft long, 39 ft wide

    b. 170 ft long, 30 ft wide

    c. 85 ft long, 60 ft wide

    d. 101 ft long, 50 ft wide

4. What is the coefficient of **x**?

$$y + 12x + 6x^2 - 8$$

5. The *Queen Elizabeth* was the largest passenger ocean liner when it was built in 1955. The *Queen Mary II*, built in 2005, surpassed the *Queen Elizabeth* in length by 101 feet. The *Titanic* was one-third the length of the *Queen Mary II*. The sum of the lengths of all three ships is 2,540 feet.

Give the length of each ship.

a._____

b._____

c._____

Name

1. Evaluate: $\dfrac{(-6)(-7)}{-3}$

2. Choose the expression to match the words.

the difference between a number cubed and three times another number is equal to seventy-seven

    ○ $x^3 - 3x = 77$

    ○ $3x - 77 = x^3$

    ○ $x^3 - 3y = 77$

3. Is the graph of this equation a straight line?

$$3y = x^2 - 1$$

4. Add or subtract the expressions.

    a) $10^3 + 3^3 =$

    b) $3\sqrt[4]{x^4} - 6\sqrt[4]{x^4}$

    c) $6\sqrt{3} + \sqrt{3}$

5. According to the *Guinness Book of Records*, the largest pumpkin pie weighed 418 lbs. Use the information in the diagram to calculate its volume.

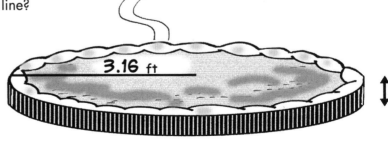

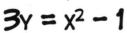

3.16 ft

3 in

1. Circle the correct solution. $\frac{1}{3}p = \frac{2}{9}$

$p = \frac{2}{27}$ $p = \frac{1}{3}$ $p = \frac{2}{3}$

2. The world's longest model train is 2,763 inches long. Would it stretch around the perimeter of a backyard that is 84 feet wide and 122 feet long?

3. Simplify: $\frac{1}{2}(y - 10) \geq x(x + 5)$

4. Which shows a correct simplification?

$(6p^2)(p^4)(q) = 6q^6 + pq$

$(6p^2)(p^4)(q) = 6p^6q$

$(6p^2)(p^4)(q) = 6p^8 + p^4q + pq$

$(6p^2)(p^4)(q) = 6pq^6$

5. The Hollywood sign in Los Angeles, California, is one of the most famous large signs in the world. Each letter is 45 feet tall.

a. What is the height of the letters in meters?

b. One letter of the alphabet is drawn at random. What is the probability that it will be one of the letters on the sign?

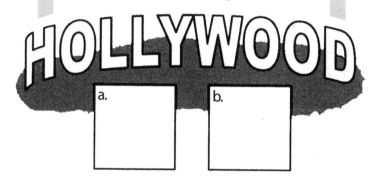

a. ☐   b. ☐

1. The biggest lollipop on record was approximately 6.5 feet wide and 10 feet tall. It was about 9 inches thick. Find its approximate surface area.

2. Simplify: $\sqrt{36 \cdot 8}$

3. Evaluate for $a = \frac{1}{3}$; $b = \frac{2}{5}$; $c = \frac{1}{4}$
$a(b + c)$

4. The variables **x** and **y** are each > 0. In all three expressions, **x** has the same value and **y** has the same value. Choose the expression with the greatest value.

$\circ (X + Y)^2$ $\circ (X + Y) + X$ $\circ \dfrac{(X - Y)^5}{(X - Y)^3}$

5. a. Approximately how much of this tea would it take to make one cup of tea?

b. Write a ratio that compares the length of the teabag to the length including the string.

WOLRD'S BIGGEST TEABAG

- length: 10 feet
- width: 3 feet
- length of string: 14 feet
- amount of tea: 15 pounds, 7 ounces
- estimated cups of tea it could make: 3,500

(HAS ANYONE SEEN THE WORLD'S LARGEST TEA CUP?)

1. A group of friends set out to make the world's largest ball of aluminum foil. After 92 days of collecting foil and adding it to the ball, their creation weighed 1,196 pounds. If they added to the ball at the same rate each day, on what day did the ball weigh 637 pounds?

2. State the slope and y-intercept for this equation.

$$y = 3x + 4$$

3. Solve for **x** if **y = –7**:

$$y^2 + 10y + 9 = 4x + 4$$

4. Write T (true) or F (false) for each statement.

___ If a < b, then a + c < b + c.

___ If a > b, then a + c > b + c.

___ If c > 0 and a > b, then ac > bc.

___ If c < o and a > b, then ac > bc.

5. Challenge Problem

Some people love the challenge of making record-sized things. Pictured below are representations of the world's largest hourglass, yo-yo, burger, bonfire, drum, and beach towel. Pay attention to the measurements that will help you figure out the size of the base for each gigantic creation.

REALLY BIG THINGS

HOURGLASS

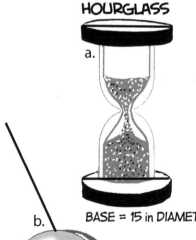

a. Write the names of these big things in order of the perimeters of their bases, from least to greatest.

b. Write the names of these big things in order of the area of their bases, from least to greatest.

BEACH TOWEL

40 ft, 5 in

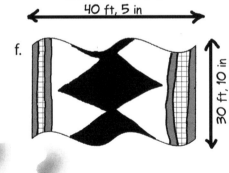

f.

30 ft, 10 in

a.

BASE = 15 in DIAMETER

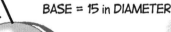

b.

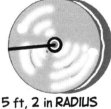

5 ft, 2 in RADIUS

YO-YO

c. **HAMBURGER**

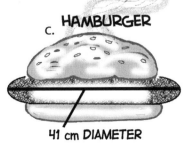

41 cm DIAMETER

d.

8 ft

10.75 ft

BONFIRE

e.

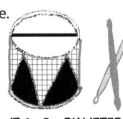

15 ft, 9 in DIAMETER

DRUM

1. The 1891 invention of the escalator has helped to move a lot of people up and down over the years. The world's longest escalator system (in Hong Kong) is 800 meters. Convert this measurement to feet.

2. Is the expression simplified correctly?

$$\frac{(x^4 \cdot x^3)}{x^2} = x^7 + x$$

3. Use words to write the expression:

$$x^2 \sqrt{12}$$

4. Solve:

$$\frac{2x - 3}{2} + \frac{x + 6}{8} = \frac{5x - 6}{8}$$

534 jumps in 24 hours

5. The parachute was invented in 1785. In 2003, Jay Stokes of the U.S. set a record for the most parachute jumps in 24 hours. In that time period, he jumped 534 times.

   a. About how much time, on average, was needed for each jump?

   b. If he could continue at the same rate, about how long would it take him to make 1,000 jumps?

1. Simplify: $|12| - |-8| + |-6|$

2. Which examples show correct factoring?

   a. $x^2 - 2x$ $x(x - 2)$

   b. $y^2 + 2y + 1$ $(y + 1)(y - 1)$

   c. $x^2 + 2x + 5x + 10$ $(x + 4)(x + 5)$

   d. $x^2 - y^2$ $(x + y)(x - y)$

3. Simplify the inequality:

   $$-6 - 4(x + 2) \le 10x$$

4. The piano, a 1709 invention, has keys of two colors. The total number of keys is 88. The number of black keys is ten more than half the number of white keys.

5. Driving in a bad storm, Charlie was grateful for the 1903 invention of windshield wipers. When he started them up, he counted 235 sweeps (both directions) in the first 2 minutes. At that rate, how many sweeps of the wipers could he expect during the entire 2-hour drive?

H O W | M A N Y | K E Y S | A R E | W H I T E ?

1. The pencil is one invention used and sold all over the world. Residents in the United States buy twenty million pencils a year.

   Write this number in scientific notation.

2. What is the HCF (highest common factor) of the terms in this expression?
$$-p^2(q - 2) + (q - 2)^2$$

3. The compact disc, invented in 1972, has a diameter of 4.75 inches and a thickness of about 0.06 inch. The surface area of a CD is about:
   ○ **17 in^2**   ○ **36 in^2**   ○ **36 in^3**   ○ **53 in^2**

4. How many *like* terms are in this expression?
$$8x^2 - 2x^3 + 5x - x^2 + y^2 - 9$$

5. Though they were invented many years apart, the pencil and the laptop computer are both tools that help writers accomplish their tasks. Follow the clues below to find the year each of these amazing instruments was invented.

Their difference is 192.
Their sum is 3782.

1. Fifteen-year old Richie Stanchowski took some money [(5 • 46) + 32 dollars] from his savings and put it to work. He bought supplies to create an invention called a Water Talkie. Now, kids all over the world can use the toy to hold underwater conversations.

   ## What is this amount of money?

2. Find the next three terms in the sequence:

   18, 32, 46, 60, 74, . . .

   _____ , _____ , _____ ,

3. Evaluate each expression.
$$12^0 \qquad 4^{-3} \qquad 12^1 \qquad 5^{-2}$$

4. Subtract:
$$-b^4 + 3b - 2b^2 + 7 \text{ from } 5b^2 + 5b + 9 + 2b^4$$

5. The computer mouse was invented in 1988. Last week, Shana found a great sale on one of the newest versions of this invention (a hot pink cordless mouse) on sale. The original price was $29.00. She paid $24.36. This total included 5% sales tax.

   What was the *discount* on the mouse?

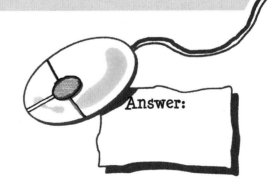

Answer:

Name

1. Is the inequality graphed correctly?

$$5 > x - 3$$

2. Luke shops for computer equipment. He has three color choices for the computer (black, silver, white), three choices for the monitor (black, silver, white), two choices for the keyboard color (silver, white), and four choices for the mouse (white, silver, red, black). How many different color combinations of the four items are possible?

3. Find the slope and y-intercept for this line:

y + 0.5 = 0.6x

Another bright idea!

4.

NUMBER OF MONTHS	27	72	38	52	10	16	65	42	44	6
NUMBER OF INVENTIONS	15	90	30	44	21	19	65	50	81	10

Make a scatter plot of this data for the number of months each of ten inventors spent trying out ideas and the number of inventions completed.

5. Challenge Problem

Read the examples. Use the information to determine the year for each of the inventions.

Invention	Year
zipper	_____
paper	_____
DVD	_____
dishwasher	_____
Velcro	_____
magnifying glass	_____
helicopter	_____
pop top can	_____
cell phone	_____

• The magnifying glass was invented 750 years before the turn of the 21st century.

• The sum of the zipper invention date and pop top can date is 3880.

• The dishwasher was invented one year less than a century and a decade before the DVD.

• Velcro was invented nine years after the helicopter.

• The pop top can was invented 1858 years after paper.

• The dishwasher came 5 decades and 3 years before the helicopter.

• The sum of Velcro and cell phone invention dates: 3927.

• The difference between dates of the DVD and the zipper inventions is 78 years.

• The invention of paper happened 20 years less than one-tenth the date of the magnifying glass.

1. In Australia, tales are told of the Bunyip, a strange creature that lurks in swamps. Thirty out of seventy-five people who claim to have seen a Bunyip describe it as half animal and half human. At this rate, how many witnesses out of 800 would describe it the same way?

2. Find the median of the data set:

$$\sqrt{121}, \ 16, \ 38, \ 19, \ 4^2, \ 23, \ 18$$

3. Simplify:

$$(3n + 6y) - (5n + 4y)$$

4. Eleven and nine tenths is what percent of eighty-five?

5. The legendary Sasquatch (Bigfoot) and the Yeti (Abominable Snowman) reputably are large creatures. Charlie makes this claim: "The Sasquatch can eat ten hamburgers per minute. His buddy, the Yeti, is less fond of meat, but still eats six burgers per minute."

   Assume Charlie's claim is true. Together, how long would it take the two creatures to devour sixty-four burgers?

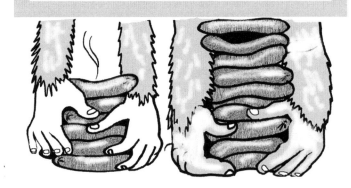

1. What is the additive inverse of the sum?

    $$(-16) + (-12)$$

    a. 28   b. 1   c. 0   d. -28

2. Simplify:

    $$\frac{36a^5b^4}{4ab}$$

3. Reports of Mothman sightings began in 1966. Legends say the creature has a wingspan three feet wider than its height.

    Write two different expressions that show this relationship. Use **w** for wingspan and **h** for height.

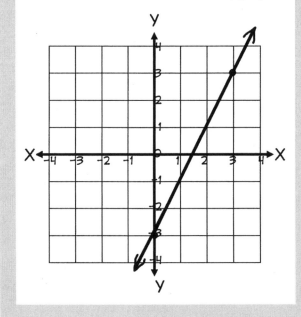

4. What is the slope of a line with this equation?

    $$2x + 5y = 16$$

5. Write an equation in slope-intercept form for the line shown on the graph.

Name

1. Simplify: $\left(\frac{6^2}{9}\right) + 4(6x - 2)$

2. Climbing in the high Himalayan Mountains at 21,000 feet altitude, British writer Charles Howard-Bury found footprints in the snow. He gave a name to the creature he thought had created them: the Abominable Snowman.

   Write this altitude in meters. *(Round to the nearest whole meter.)*

3. Evaluate: $y = 4^x$ for $x = 3$

   ○ 256 ○ 64 ○ –16 ○ 1024

4. Solve the system: $3x + 2y = 6$
   $x + y = 0$

   a. (6, 2)   b. (6, –2)   c. (–6, 6)

5. The giant clam is the largest living bivalve mollusk. Though it looks strange and has the reputation of being a "man-eating clam," there are no verified reports of any deaths caused by the clam. The clam has a diameter as great as five feet.

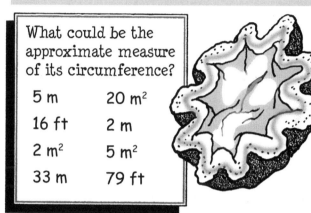

What could be the approximate measure of its circumference?

5 m	20 m²
16 ft	2 m
2 m²	5 m²
33 m	79 ft

Name

1. Simplify: $\dfrac{[-36a + 6 + (-6)]}{6}$

2. Write in scientific notation: **0.000673**

3. Simplify: $(8p - 4) - (12p - 3)$

4. Since 1975, hundreds of witnesses claim to have seen the Jersey Devil, a strange dog-like beast rumored to roam New Jersey pine forests. The same number claims to have seen Bigfoot in the forests of the northern U.S. and Canada from 1975 to 2005. If the Jersey Devil had been seen at the same rate as Bigfoot, how many Devils would have been spotted from 1735–2005?

   Jersey Devil Sightings 1735 – 2005

5. The Chupacabra is a creature said to inhabit parts of Latin America. The table shows some data about sightings of the lizard-like legend.

   If the number of sightings continued to follow this pattern, what would have been the numbers in 2007 and 2008?

   Chupacabra Sightings 2007 - 2008

Year	Sightings
2001	87
2002	94
2003	101
2004	108
2005	115
2006	122

Name

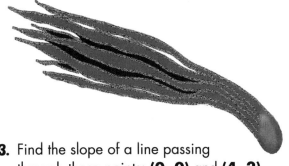

1. Choose the correct answer.

The Dana octopus squid (a monster-sized creature), blinds and stuns its prey with arms that glow! The largest specimen caught weighed 135 pounds. This weight is closest to

○ **260 kg**   ○ **1350 oz**   ○ **80 kg**

○ **6100 g**   ○ **61,000 g**   ○ **610 g**

3. Find the slope of a line passing through these points: **(0, 0)** and **(4, 2)**.

2. Solve:

$$-3x + 7 \leq 10$$

4. Factor:

$$3xy^2 + 6x^2y^2 - 3xy$$

5. Challenge Problem

a. Complete the table to find three points to graph.

b. Solve the equation **y = 2x − 4** by graphing.

c. Explain in your own words what "solve" means.

d. Give the solution to the equation:_____

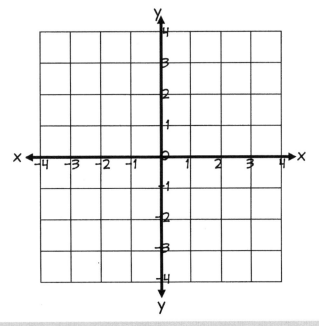

y = 2x - 4

x	y	(x, y)
1		
3		
0		

1. The Great Pyramid of Giza is the only surviving of the Seven Wonders of the Ancient World. It was built with two million blocks of stone, each weighing two tons.

Write the total weight as an exponential number.

2. Simplify: $\dfrac{8x^4y^8}{2x^7y^3}$

3. Write the following equation in standard form for a linear equation:

$$44 = y - 50 - 2x$$

4. Solve the system:

$$2x + y = 16$$
$$y + 2 = x$$

5. The Great Wall of China was built in 221 B.C. to keep out invading armies. A group of hikers intends to travel the entire distance of the wall—3,948 miles—walking at a rate of two mph for eight hours a day.

At this rate, can they cover the entire distance in three months?

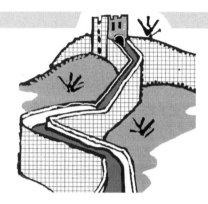

1. What operation should be done first?

$$7(p + 6) - 9 + 3 = 75$$

2. Solve: $(n + 4)^2 - 36 = 0$

   a. 2 and –2   c. 10 and 2

   b. 2 and –10   d. –2 and –10

3. Which expression is equal to six?

   a. negative seventeen minus negative eleven

   b. the product of negative seven and five plus forty-one

   c. two to the seventh power divided by two to the third pow

4. Evaluate for $p = 6$ and $q = 0.5$.

$$2p^2 - 12q + q^2$$

5. Angkor Wat is a temple that was built in the early 12th Century. It was surrounded by a wall, an apron of lawn **30 m** wide, and a moat **190 m** wide. Today, its ruins are a prime attraction for visitors to Cambodia.

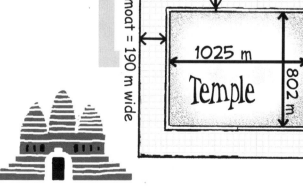

apron = 30 m wide

moat = 190 m wide

1025 m

Temple

802 m

Find the surface area of water in the moat.

1. Which is true of **(–30)(3)?**

The product is the reciprocal of $\frac{1}{90}$.

The product is the reciprocal of $-\frac{1}{90}$.

The product is the reciprocal of –90.

2. Evaluate: $(5^6)(5^{-4}) =$ ☐

3. The slope of a line passing through **(2, 6)** and **(5, –1)** can be found by using which ratio?

  a. $\frac{6-(-1)}{2-5}$ c. $\frac{5-6}{1-2}$

  b. $\frac{2-5}{6-1}$ d. $\frac{6-5}{2-1}$

4. Simplify: $8a^2 - 4(3a^2 + 9)$

5. Rosa is getting ready to visit Machu Picchu, the ancient Incan fortress city in the Andes Mountains of Peru. About 3,000 steps connect the different levels of the site. To prepare, she is running up the steps to the second floor in her house. Each step has a six-inch rise, and she has climbed 500 steps a day for 30 days.

She wants to climb a total of five miles in 60 days. How many steps a day will she need to climb for the next 30 days to reach that goal?

1. The Alhambra, an ancient fortress in southern Spain, covers an area in square meters that can be described this way: a product of ten to the fourth power and fourteen and two tenths.

Write this expression. ➡ ☐

2. Finish the equation to show the commutative property.

$$b^2 + c + a^2b =$$

3. Solve: $-8x + 33 = 5x - 3$

4. Solve for **x** and graph the solution.

$$x - 7 > -4$$

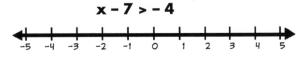

5. The chart shows time spent traveling by each member of a travel club. For the set of data, find . . .

  a. the mean

  b. the median

  c. the range

  d. the mode

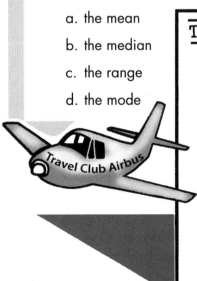

Travel Times
16 hours
66 hours
123 hours
13 hours
44 hours
16 hours
87 hours
39 hours
55 hours

Name

1. Solve the proportions.

a. $\dfrac{4}{m} = \dfrac{64}{112}$ b. $\dfrac{3}{11} = \dfrac{42}{n}$

2. The Colosseum was the largest amphitheater constructed by the Roman Empire. It was completed in 80 AD. How many full decades have passed since that time?

3. Is the equation in standard form of a linear equation?

$$5x - y = 12$$

4. It took 20,000 workers 22 years to build the Taj Mahal, an elegant mausoleum in India. Assume that each worker worked an average of ten hours a day, three hundred days a year. The total number of worker hours on this project would be closest to:

○ 4.4×10^7 ○ 13.2×10^8

○ 1.0×10^6 ○ $2,000^3$

○ 1.32×10^9 ○ 4.4×10^8

5. Challenge Problem

The Great Pyramid has a square base. Each side of the base has a length of 755.5 feet. If the volume of the Great Pyramid is 85,600,000 cubic feet, what is its approximate height?

Use the formula for the volume of a pyramid.

$$V = \tfrac{1}{3} B h \text{ (where } B = \text{area of the base)}$$

When you've solved this problem, see if you can solve the **riddle of the Sphinx**.

THE GREAT SPHINX, WHICH SITS NEAR THE GREAT PYRAMID, IS A MAJOR ATTRACTION AT GIZA, EGYPT. IT IS A HUGE CREATION WITH THE HEAD OF A HUMAN AND THE BODY OF A LION. THERE WERE NUMEROUS SPHINXES IN EGYPT AND GREECE. ACCORDING TO MYTHOLOGY, A SPHINX SAT OUTSIDE OF THEBES AND ASKED A RIDDLE OF EVERYONE WHO PASSED BY:

What goes on four legs in the morning, on two legs at noon, and on three legs in the evening?

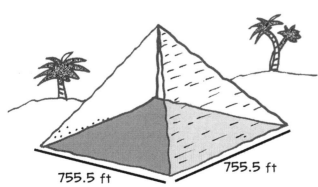

755.5 ft   755.5 ft

BELIEVE IT OR NOT!
The body of a 70 kg person contains 7 mg of arsenic.

1. How much arsenic would you expect to find in the body of an **85 kg** person?

2. Simplify: x^{-3}

3. Find the opposite of $-(n - m)$.

4. Do these points lie on a straight line?

A (–3, 5)   **B** (6, –4)   **C** (0, –2)

5. A group of pet owners were surveyed about the sleeping habits of their pets. They reported a total of sixty-seven pets that snore. If the fact (below) is true of this group, how many pets were considered in the survey?

Wacky Fact
According to pet owners, seven percent of all pets snore.

1.

Did You Know
A dime has 118 ridges.

How many ridges are on $688 worth of dimes?

2. Change each to an exponential expression:

$\sqrt{x} =$ $\sqrt[3]{12} =$

3. Write this expression:

Six times a number divided by four times the sum of another number and three.

4. Evaluate for **x = 22** and **y = –10**.

$$\frac{x+y}{2} + \frac{x-y}{8}$$

5. Write a number in scientific notation to represent each fact.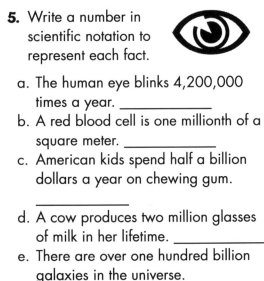

a. The human eye blinks 4,200,000 times a year. _____

b. A red blood cell is one millionth of a square meter. _____

c. American kids spend half a billion dollars a year on chewing gum. _____

d. A cow produces two million glasses of milk in her lifetime. _____

e. There are over one hundred billion galaxies in the universe. _____

f. Dunkin' Donuts sells 2.3 billion donuts a year. _____

1. Factor: $a^3b + ab^2 - 3ab$

2. What is the difference?

three times the cube root of a number (x) minus six times the cube root of the same number

3. Simplify: $\dfrac{12x^4y^3}{2xy^2}$

4. How many bees does it take to make a cup of honey?

(Conversion factor: 1 C = 48 tsp)

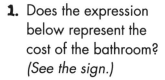

CURIOUS FACT!
- A bee produces $\frac{1}{12}$ teaspoon of honey in its lifetime.

INTERESTING FACTS . . .
- Wrigley's chewing gum was the first product to be scanned with a bar code. This was on June 26, 1974.
- The most overdue book ever tracked was borrowed from Sidney Sussex College in Cambridge, England. It was returned 288 years later.

5. Use the information on the sign above to answer the questions:

a. How many days ago was the chewing gum scanned?

b. If the library's overdue charge was five cents a day, about how much was the fine on the book?

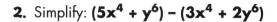

1. Does the expression below represent the cost of the bathroom? *(See the sign.)*

$$(\sqrt{49})(\sqrt[3]{125})(10^5)$$

SHOCKING FACT!
The most expensive bathroom on record cost $3.5 million to build.

2. Simplify: $(5x^4 + y^6) - (3x^4 + 2y^6)$

3. Evaluate for **c = 6** and **d = –4**.

$$\frac{c^2}{(d+2)^3}$$

4. Solve: $-10n + n - (-15n) + 12 = 27n$

5. Use the fact on the sign below to help solve the problem.

Assume that each of those hot dogs was served with 5 grams of mustard. How many 350-gram bottles of mustard would have been purchased to do the job of spicing up the dogs?

(Round to nearest whole number.)

SURPRISING FACT
In the year 2000, Americans consumed 20 billion hot dogs.

Wacky Fact

NINETY-FIVE PERCENT OF PEOPLE WHO EAT PEANUT BUTTER AND JELLY SANDWICHES PUT THE PEANUT BUTTER ON THE BREAD BEFORE THE JELLY.

1. A group of 575 people begins making peanut butter and jelly sandwiches. How many people do you expect would put the jelly on the bread before the peanut butter? *(Round to the nearest whole number.)*

2. Which has the greater value if **x** and **y** have the same value in each expression and **x > 0** and **y > 2**?

$$\sqrt{81x^2} \qquad 2x^2y \qquad -xy^2$$

3. Is **n = 5** the correct solution to the equation below?

$$4\sqrt[3]{64} + n^2 = -6n + 71$$

4. Imagine the image of the triangle if it were reflected over the **y-axis**. Describe the coordinates for the three vertices.

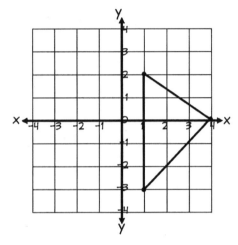

5. Challenge Problem

Strange, but Perhaps, True!

According to some sources, the average (4 ounce) chocolate bar contains **8** insect legs!

Some people do not like their chocolate "bugged." They feel two insect legs per bar is plenty. How much pure chocolate (if they could get it) would confectioners have to mix with 20 pounds of the "bugged" chocolate to get only two legs in a bar?

1. Comic book figure Captain America carries only one weapon—a shield. It has a diameter of 2.5 feet and weighs 12 pounds. Find the area of one side of the shield.

2. Simplify: $x^{\frac{1}{2}} \bullet x^{\frac{1}{2}}$

3. $2x^2 + x - 2 = 0$

In the equation above, find the coefficients of . . .
   a) the x^2 **term** _____
   b) the **x term** _____

4. Find the equation of the straight line with a slope of **2** through the point **(–3, 5)**.

5. Batman and Robin love to practice sliding down a steel cable to the ground from a tall building.

The building is 400 feet high. About how much cable will they need to land 300 feet away from the base of the building?

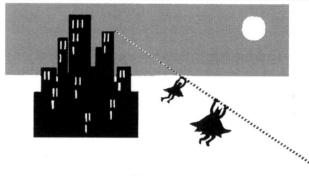

1. What is the reciprocal of x^{-3}?

2. Factor the polynomial:
$$2c^6 - 4c^3 + 6c^2$$

3. What are the **x** and **y intercepts** of the line?
$$y = -3x + 12$$

4. The volume (V) of a right rectangular prism can be found with the formula **V = lwh** (where **l** is the length, **w** is the width, and **h** is the height).

If $l = xy$, $w = 2xy$, and $h = 3xyz$, what is the volume?

5. Pepe le Peux, famed cartoon skunk, has fallen in love with a cute feline whom he has mistaken for a skunk (again)! Curiously enough, the feline has recently had a chance encounter with a paintbrush (loaded with white paint) that fell from a scaffolding above her sidewalk promenade. This has given her a white "stripe" of the shape and dimensions shown.

IF THE PAINT DISINTEGRATES AT THE RATE OF ONE SQUARE INCH A DAY, HOW LONG WILL IT BE BEFORE PEPE SEES THE WHOLE TRUTH AND LOSES INTEREST IN THE FELINE?

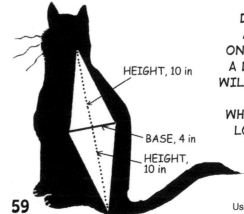

HEIGHT, 10 in
BASE, 4 in
HEIGHT, 10 in

WEDNESDAY WEEK 19 _____ MATH PRACTICE

Name

1. Recently, a 1940 comic book featuring the first appearance of *The Spectre* sold for a large amount of money. To find the dollar amount, evaluate the expression:

$$2^5 \cdot 3 \cdot 5^3 \cdot 7$$

2. Simplify: $\dfrac{x^3 y^2 z^5}{x^3 y z^4}$

3. What is the intersection of these sets?

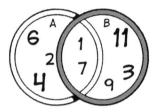

4. Garfield can eat a big lasagna in $\frac{1}{2}$ hour and two Italian food lovers can eat the same lasagna in $1\frac{1}{2}$ hours. How long will it take them to polish off the lasagna if they all eat it together?

5. Write an equation for each line: a and b.

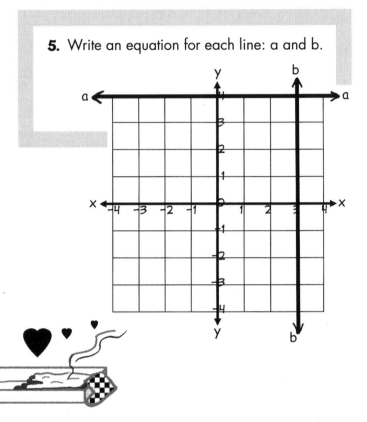

THURSDAY WEEK 19 _____ MATH PRACTICE

Name

1. The most valuable American comic book is *Action Comics No. 1*, published in June, 1938. Its value is $440,000.

The prime factors of this number are **2, 5,** and **11.** How many of each make up the prime factorization of **440,000?**

2. Simplify: $\dfrac{a^4 b^7 c^3}{a^3 b^3 c^3}$

3. Find the product: **(2xy) (3xz) (4xw)**

4. Write the interval **2 ≤ x ≤ 6** using the absolute value symbol and one ≤ sign.

5. Japan is the world's leading comic-reading nation. The proceeds from manga comics represent 40% of the income from all printed material sold in the country. In the 1990s, yearly sales of manga comics were about $5.5 billion each year.

How much (on average) did the Japanese spend on printed materials each year in the 1990s? Write the answer in scientific notation.

1. Maria's dad bought one of the first *Ghost Rider* comics in 1973 for 50¢. Today, the comic book that holds the tale of Ghost Rider's first appearance is worth $300. What is the percent of increase in the worth?

2. Assume **y ≠ 0**.

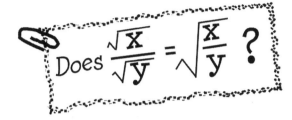

Does $\dfrac{\sqrt{x}}{\sqrt{y}} = \sqrt{\dfrac{x}{y}}$?

3. If the perimeter of the trapezoid is 49 inches, what are the lengths of its sides?

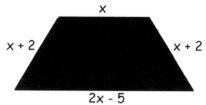

x

$x + 2$ $x + 2$

$2x - 5$

4. Simplify:

$$\frac{39rs}{52rs}$$

5. Challenge Problem

THE INTEGER CODE

Detective Deirdre DeDuce is both smart and beautiful. But her nemesis, 'Wrongnumber' Jackie Johnson is sure the detective will never figure out the math puzzle he uses to hide his stolen loot in a safety deposit box. He brazenly gives her the clues to decode the secret number.

Can you figure out the number before she does?

I'll stump this detective, for sure.

Figure this out if you can! For **three** consecutive integers, **twice** the third is **21** more than **three** times the sum of the first and third.

I **love** a good challenge.

Then, multiply the integers together and divide by a **negative two**.

Heh, heh, heh.

I think I know the answer. Have you got it yet?

Answer:

1. Speedskaters reach amazing speeds. To find the top speed as of 2006 (in seconds) for the 500-meter race, evaluate this expression:

$$1177.86^{\frac{1}{2}}$$

2. What is the next number in the pattern?

$3^0, 3^1, 3^2, 3^3,$ _____

3. The Pythagorean Theorem applies to only which type of figure? _____

4. In 1988, ice skater Martinus Kuiper skated 339.67 mi to set the world record for the greatest ice-skating distance in 24 hrs. At this rate, how far did he skate in six hours?

5. Graph $y = |x|$ on the grid below.

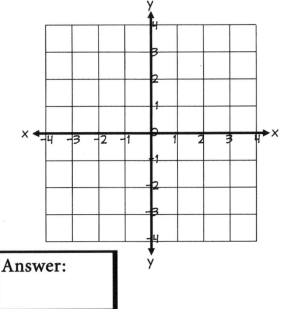

Answer:

1. Simplify: $(x^3)^5$

2. Vreni Schneider of Switzerland has won more world cup ski races in one season than any other woman in the world. Five less than her record squared is 164. What is her record?

3. What is the slope of the equation?

$$y = \frac{2}{3}x - 1$$

4. Graph the compound inequality on the line below:

$x < 2$ *and* $x > -3$

```
<———+————+————+————+————+————+————+————+————+————+————>
    -5   -4   -3   -2   -1   0    1    2    3    4    5
```

5. The Cresta Run bobsled course is 3,977 ft long with a drop of 514 ft. What is the average slope of the run?

1. To find the top speed for a bobsled, solve the following equation for **x** = 20 mph:

$$y = 2x + 40$$

2. Is $\left(\frac{a}{b}\right)^n = \frac{a^n}{b^n}$ for all integers **n** and nonzero **a** and **b**?

3. The longest alpine ski race takes place on the Inferno course in Switzerland that stretches 9.8 miles. The fastest time to complete the course is 13 min, 54 sec. On average, how fast did the person go (in mph) who set the record?

4. What is the union of the following sets?

5. Which is the graph of **y = |x + 1|** ?

a.
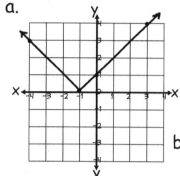

b.

1. Downhill skiers can reach great speeds—even up to 100 mph.

What is this in feet per second?

2. Write 3^{-3} as a simple fraction.

3. What is the y-intercept of the line represented by this equation?

$$y = -\tfrac{1}{2}x + 4$$

4. This is a graph of which compound inequality?

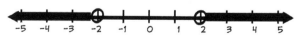

   a. **x > 2** AND **x > −2**

   b. **x > 2** OR **x < −2**

   c. **x < −2**

5. How long does it take a rock falling from a vertical cliff to reach the speed of a downhill skier, skiing at the speed in problem #1? *(Round your answer to the nearest tenth of a second.)*

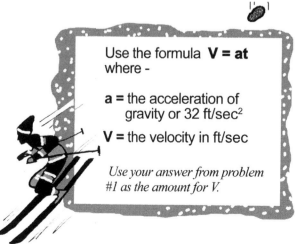

Use the formula **V = at** where -

a = the acceleration of gravity or 32 ft/sec^2

V = the velocity in ft/sec

Use your answer from problem #1 as the amount for V.

1. Evaluate:

$$4[5 (13 - 2\{6\})] - 19$$

2. Solve the following system:

$$x + y = 10$$

$$x - y = 6$$

3. The longest ice-skating race on record *(The Elfstedentocht)* covers 124.27 miles. The women's record time is 5 hr, 48 min, 8 sec. What is the average speed (in mph) for the woman who set this record?

4. Graph the compound inequality:

$$x \leq -1 \text{ OR } x \geq 1$$

5. Challenge Problem

The grid shows a cross section of a downhill ski course. Each section is labeled with a letter. Calculate the slope of each section.

A. HEARTSTOP DROP_____   D. LAST CHANCE RUN_____

B. EASY STREET_____   E. RAINBOW CANYON_____

C. SUNSHINE AVENUE_____   F. HOME STRETCH_____

Name

1. The thick-billed murre can dive deeper into the ocean than any other flying bird: 690 feet. Convert this measurement to meters. *(Round to the nearest meter.)*

2. Simplify: $\left(\dfrac{x}{y}\right)^{-2} =$

3. How would you read the following compound interest formula out loud?

$$T = P(1 + i)^n$$

4. Which is the graph of $y = |x| + 1$?

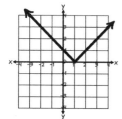 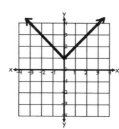

5. Take the deepest dive of an elephant seal (ft) and add it to the deepest seawater scuba dive (ft) by diver John Bennett. The result is 6,027 ft. Two times the elephant seal's depth minus Bennett's depth is 9,024 ft.

a. Deepest dive by an elephant seal = [____] feet

b. Deepest seawater scuba dive (by John Bennett) = [____] feet

Name

1. The sum of the lengths of two sides of any triangle is _____ than the length of the third side.

2. Evaluate: $2^2 \cdot 5^3 \cdot 37$ to find the depth in feet (undersea) where the deepest sponges grow.

3. What is the slope of the line through the points **(1, 1)** and **(2, 2)**?

4. If you deposit $1,000 in a bank account, what will be the total amount in the account after 20 years at an annual interest rate of 6%?

[Hint: Use the formula **T = P(1 + i)ⁿ** where
T = total, P = principal, i = interest rate,
and n = number of years]

A bay with 67,000 crabs starts losing 5% of its population each year.

5. Refer to the information on the sign above to answer these questions.

a. Is the statement an example of exponential growth or exponential decay?

b. If this loss continues at the same rate, how many crabs will be left in the bay after ten years?

WEDNESDAY WEEK 21 _____ MATH PRACTICE
Name

1. The vampire squid has a body length of six inches and eyes one inch in diameter. This gives it the largest eye to body ratio of any animal. If you were five feet tall, how large would your eyes have to be to have the same ratio?

2. True or false?

   A graph whose equation is of the form $y = ax^2 + bx + c$ ($a \neq 0$) is a parabola.

3. Define: y-intercept

4. Solve for **x**:

   $-4x > 6x + 25$

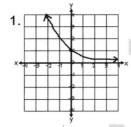

1.

2.

3.

4.

5. Match each graph below with the situation it models:

   a. exponential increase

   b. linear decrease

   c. exponential decay

   d. linear increase

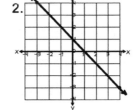

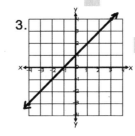

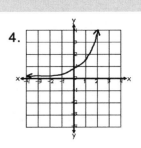

THURSDAY WEEK 21 _____ MATH PRACTICE
Name

1. The longest organism in the world is a jellyfish measuring up to 160 ft. The length of an Olympic swimming pool is 50 m. Write a ratio comparing the length of the jellyfish to the length of the pool.

2. Simplify this by writing without parentheses:

   $$\left(\frac{3}{2}x\right)^4$$

3. The deepest shipwreck is the *SS Rio Grande*, which lies 18,904 ft beneath the surface of the South Atlantic Ocean. Round this to the nearest hundred and express it in scientific notation.

4. The edge of one cube is **z** inches long. Another cube is three times as long. Write an expression for
   a. the volume of the first cube
   b. the volume of the second cube

Erin buys **six** prolific tropical fish. Every month the population **doubles**. Assume she has room for the new fish and the food to feed them.

5. Use the information above to help solve these problems.
   a. How many fish will there be at the end of four months?
   b. How many fish will there be at the end of a year?

Name

1. Write an expression for the area of the figure below and a second expression for its perimeter.

x

y

2. A card is drawn randomly from a deck of 52 playing cards.

    a. Find the probability that it is an ace.

    b. Find the probability that it is an ace or a queen.

3. The perimeter of the triangle is 120 feet. Find the length of each side.

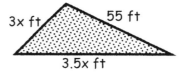

3x ft   55 ft

3.5x ft

4. What is the volume of the aquarium (below) in cubic feet?

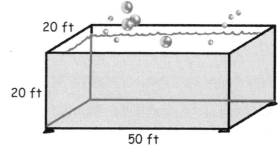

20 ft

20 ft

50 ft

5. Challenge Problem

Jordan is on the sea floor at a depth of 1,010 ft. She wants to proceed to a sunken treasure chest that is 2,000 ft away, but an elephant seal bars her way. Therefore, she goes a distance **x** in the direction from **A** to **B** and another distance **x** in the direction **B** to **C**, making a right angle at **B**.

Calculate the distance scuba diver Jordan has to go while keeping an eye on the seal.

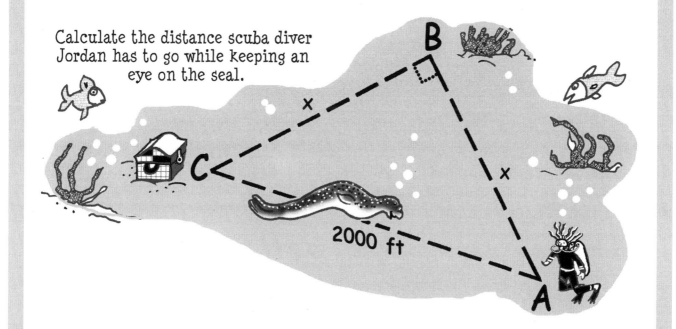

1. Kevin Cook of the USA has collected a record-setting number of dice.

    Evaluate: $3^4 \cdot 137$ to find out how many individual dice he owns.

2. When $x = 3$, what is the value of

$$\frac{(4x)^8}{(4x)^5}?$$

3. What is the slope of the line $3x + y = 6$?

4. Terry Sanderson (UK) collected 1,815 hand towels, which could cover 2,046.8 sq ft if she arranged the towels in a square. What would be the perimeter of this square? *(Round to the nearest foot.)*

5. a. Graph $y = |x|$ and $y = -|x|$ on the same coordinate grid.

   b. What effect does the negative sign have on the graph of $y = |x|$?

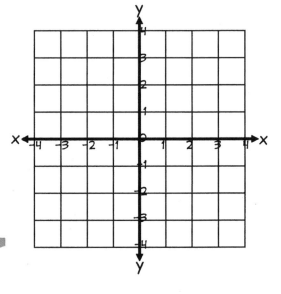

1. Walter Cavanagh from the U.S. has collected 1,497 credit cards, worth $1.7 million in credit. On average, how much credit does Walter have per card?

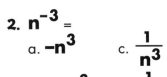

2. $n^{-3} =$
   a. $-n^3$ c. $\dfrac{1}{n^3}$

   b. $(-n)^3$ d. $\dfrac{1}{n^{-3}}$

3. Does the parabola $y = x^2$ open up or down?

4. a. Write the function $y = x^2 - x - 12$ in factored form.

   b. What are the zeros of the polynomial function in a (above)?

5. I. M. Dusty collects dryer lint. He has 10,000 pounds of lint, and has stopped collecting. However, moths are consuming 5% of his lint per year. How many pounds will he have left in twenty years? *(Round to the nearest pound.)*

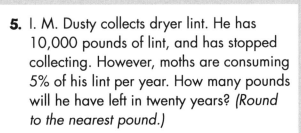

Give your solution.
Explain how you solved the problem:

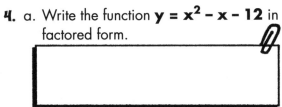

1. Anita Cash stacked her collection of sugar cubes, one on top of another, into a column 55 inches tall. If each cube was .015625 inches^3 in volume, how many cubes were in the stack?

2. Solve: $(x - 21)^2 = 100$ by taking square roots.

3. Does the equation below model exponential growth or decay?

$$y = ag^x \text{ where } g > 1$$

4. Graph the solution set of $|x| = 4$ on the number line.

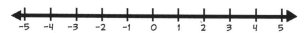

5. Bernd Sikora of Germany collects potato chip bags.

   a. The area of the triangle below multiplied by the number of bags in Bernd's collection equals 5,928. How many bags does he have?

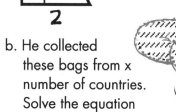

   b. He collected these bags from x number of countries. Solve the equation below to find the number of countries.

$$\frac{x}{20} \cdot 2^2 = .5375$$

1. Evaluate: $2^4 \cdot 233$ to find the number of airplane sick bags in Nick Vermeulen has collected from 802 different airlines.

2. Simplify: $(3x - 5)(2x + 3)$

3. In the polynomial $-6x^2 + 2x - 3$, what is the coefficient of the **x** term?

4. What is the distance between the two points: **A = (−4, 3)** and **B = (1, −5)**? *Round your answer to the nearest tenth.*

   Answer:

5. The sum of these two collections (below) is 6,539, while two times the number of ducks plus three times the number of gum packs equals 18,178.

   a. How many ducks?

   b. How many gum packs?

CURIOUS COLLECTIONS

Charlotte Lee holds the record for the largest rubber duck collection.

Steve Fletcher holds the world record for the largest collection of packs of gum.

1. Dalton Stevens, the "Button King of Bishopville," is a chronic insomniac. He decorates objects with buttons to keep from being bored during sleepless nights. He has a collection of 439,000 different buttons. Express this number in scientific notation.

2. The area of the shaded part of the rectangle is 46. What is **x**?

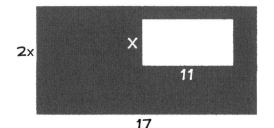

3. Does the parabola $y = -x^2$ open up or down?

4. Does $|x - 1| = -2$ have a solution set?

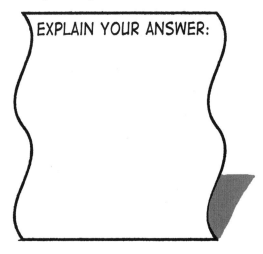

EXPLAIN YOUR ANSWER:

5. Challenge Problem

Ralph collects beetles.
He has **15,625** species already.

a. Ralph's collection doubles every year. If there are one million species of beetles, how long would it take him to collect one of each kind?

b. Unfortunately, there are only 350,000 different species of beetles in the world. How long would it take Ralph to collect every one?

About $4\frac{1}{2}$ years? About 8 years? About 2 years? About $3\frac{1}{2}$ years?

MONDAY WEEK 23 _____   MATH PRACTICE
Name

1. Actress Julia Roberts has starred in 33 movies since 1987. These movies have taken in billions of dollars. Twice the amount earned by these movies minus $89 billion is $5,789 billion. What amount have her movies earned?

2. Solve: $(x - 3^2) = 25$ by taking square roots.

3. What is the slope of the following line?

$$y = 100 - 4x$$

4. The world's smallest commercial theater (Rome, Italy) has 63 seats. Its dimensions are 16.4 ft by 8.2 ft. Assume the seats go right up to the screen and there are no aisles.

   How many square feet are left for each seat?

5. a. Graph $y = |x|$ and $y = |x - 2|$ on the same coordinate grid.

   b. What effect does the 2 have when subtracted from the original function?

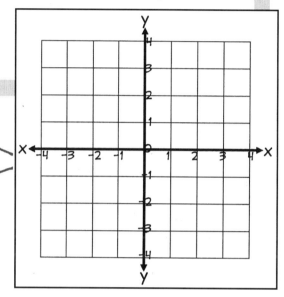

TUESDAY WEEK 23 _____   MATH PRACTICE
Name

1. The most successful movie musical, *Grease*, took in $387,713,610 at the box office. Round this to the nearest million dollars. Then write the number in scientific notation.

2. Write without negative exponents: $3x^{-2}y^{-4}$

3. a. Write the function $y = x^2 + x - 20$ in factored form.

   b. What are the zeros of this polynomial function (above)?

4. Does the following parabola open up or down?

$$y = x^2 + 2x + 6$$

5. Japan has the highest movie ticket prices in the world. India has the lowest.

   Twice the price in Japan minus five times the price in India is $20.60. Thirty cents less than three times the lowest price is thirty cents. What are the prices of tickets in the two countries?

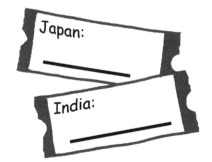

Japan:

India:

1. Iceland has the highest movie theater attendance of any country. In 2004, each person averaged 5.45 movie theater visits. The population of Iceland that year was 280,798. What was the total number of theater tickets sold in Iceland that year?

2. Factor: $x^2 + 5x + 6$

3. The equation $y = ag^x$ (where $0 < g < 1$) models:

   a. exponential growth   c. linear decrease

   b. exponential decay   d. linear increase

4. a. Graph $y = |x|$ and $y = |x| - 2$ on the same coordinate grid.

   b. What effect does subtracting 2 have on the original function?

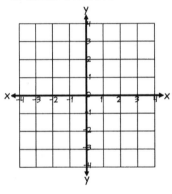

5. Julie is the manager of concessions at a small movie theater. Together, she and her helper Hank earned $100 when she worked an 8-hour shift and Hank worked 6 hours. Had each received $2 an hour more, they would have made $128 between the two of them. Find the hourly wage for each worker.

Moonlight Theater
Employees'
Hourly Wage:

$ _____ **Julie**

$ _____ **Hank**

1. The sum of the ages of the oldest and youngest Oscar nominees is 96. The difference between their ages is 78. Find their ages in years.

> **Oldest Oscar nominee:**
> *Gloria Stuart (for **Titanic**)*
>
> **Youngest Oscar nominee:**
> *Jackie Cooper (for **Skippy**)*

2. Simplify: $(2x - 2)(2x + 4)$

3. What is the probability of choosing an orange ball out of a bag containing only green balls?

4. Graph the solution set of $|x - 2| = 3$ on the number line.

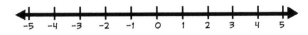

5. The movie theater manager stirs up his own mixture of popcorn. One of his concoctions combines popcorn worth $1.20 a pound and popcorn worth $1.80. It has a total value of $57.00. If each grade's value were increased by $.50, the new value for the mixture would be $74.50.

   Find the number of pounds of each grade of popcorn used in this mixture.

1. Sally usually eats her super big container of popcorn in one and a half hours, and Sam usually eats the same size box in a half hour. How fast are they likely to eat one together?

2. Does the parabola $y = -2x^2 + 4x - 6$ open up or down?

3. What is the distance between the two points **A = (−5, 3)** and **B = (2, −4)**?

4. If a large chocolate-covered malt ball is a sphere with a radius of $\frac{1}{4}$ in, what is its volume?

5. Challenge Problem

Follow the clues to complete the puzzle.

Across

5 empty set
6 longest side of a right triangle
8 polynomial with two terms
10 middle value in a set of data
11 a special case for which a pattern is false
12 a symbol that can be replaced by any one of a set of numbers
13 whole numbers and their opposites
14 two lines with the same slope are _____

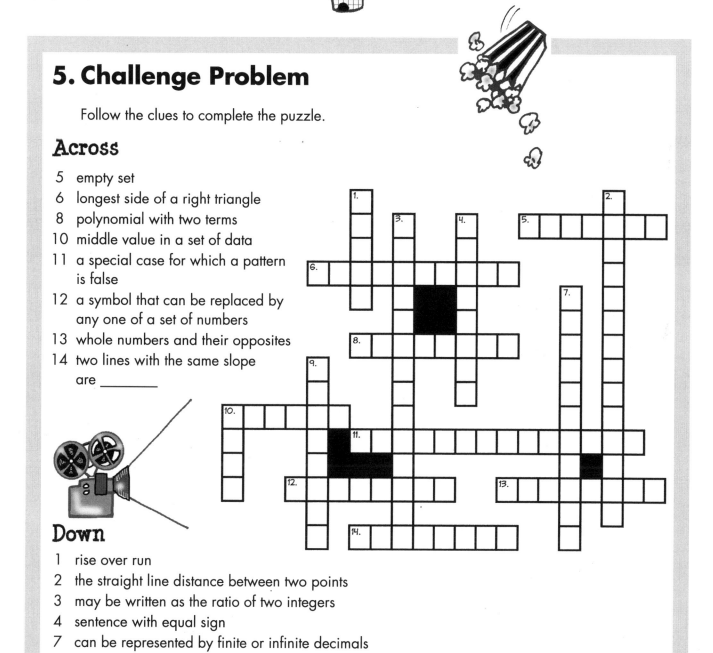

Down

1 rise over run
2 the straight line distance between two points
3 may be written as the ratio of two integers
4 sentence with equal sign
7 can be represented by finite or infinite decimals
9 one part of the four parts of the coordinate plane
10 value(s) occurring most often in data set

1. On Earth, a bull African elephant weighs about 5.5 tons. The ratio of Earth's gravity to Jupiter's gravity is 1 : 2.55. How much would the elephant weigh on Jupiter?

2. Factor completely: $7x^2y + 14x^2$

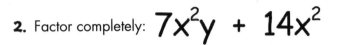

3. A _____ is a whole number that has no whole number factors except one and itself.

4. Solve for **z**:

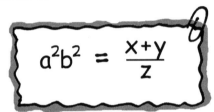

$$a^2b^2 = \frac{x+y}{z}$$

5. Dennis Tito, first tourist in space, paid $20 million for his trip aboard Russian spacecraft *Soyuz TM–32* in 2001. He spent almost 8 days in space, orbiting Earth 128 times.

   a. The diameter of Earth is 12,756 km. If Tito was in orbit 100 km above Earth, how far did he travel while orbiting? *(Round to the nearest kilometer.)*

   b. How much did he pay per kilometer?

1. Mercury is 4880 km in diameter. Express Mercury's radius in meters using scientific notation.

2. What is the square of two-thirds?

3. A situation in which the original amount is repeatedly multiplied by a growth factor between zero and one is called _____.

4. Solve for **f**: **E = hf**

5. If light travels at 186,000 miles per second, how far (in miles) does light travel in a light year? (Express your answer in scientific notation.)

Tell how you solved the problem.

1. The Sun is 92 million miles from the Earth, while the moon is 236,000 miles from the Earth. How many times farther away is the Sun than the moon? (Express your answer in scientific notation.)

2. Simplify:
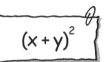
$$(x + y)^2$$

3. The nth power of a number **x** is ____.

4. Graph all solutions to the inequality:

$$-3 \leq x \leq 5$$

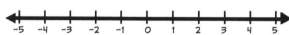

5. The Sun is moving about 230 kilometers per second and takes about 230 years to circle the galaxy once. This is a *Galactic Year.* If the Earth is 12 billion years old, how old is it in Galactic Years?

   a. about 100
   b. about 75
   c. about 52
   d. about 15
   e. none of the above

1. Evaluate: $2^4 \cdot 3^2 \cdot 5$ to find the number of fruit flies rocketed into space in 1973 aboard the *Space Lab.*

2. Factor: $$x^2 - y^2$$

3. The point (0, 0) on the coordinate plane is called _____

   a. the x-intercept
   b. the origin
   c. the y-intercept
   d. the first quadrant

4. Represent the area of a square where a side is **5 – 5s**.

If you weigh 100 pounds on Earth, you would weigh only 17 pounds on the moon.

5. Use the information from the sign above to help solve these problems.

   a. What would you weigh on the moon if you weigh 130 pounds on the Earth?
   b. Your little Chihuahua dog weighs 1 pound on the Earth. How much will he weigh on the moon if he gets the honor of being the first moon Chihuahua?

1. About how many times faster than sound is light?

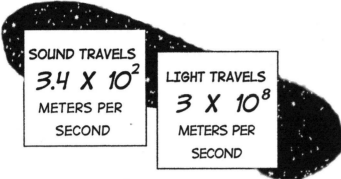

SOUND TRAVELS
3.4×10^2
METERS PER SECOND

LIGHT TRAVELS
3×10^8
METERS PER SECOND

3. Square:

$$\frac{1}{v^8}$$

4. Find the product:

$$xy(z^3 + 1)(z^3 - 1)$$

2. Solve for m_2:

$$F = G\frac{m_1 m_2}{d^2}$$

The Earth has an average density of 5500 kg/m³.

Density is given by the formula
$$D = \frac{M}{V}$$
where **M** is the mass and **V** is the volume.

The Sun is 330,000 times heavier than the Earth, which weighs about 6×10^{24} kg.

5. Challenge Problem

Use the facts and formula at the left to solve the problems below.

a. Calculate the average density of the Sun in kg/m³.

   (Remember: the volume of a sphere is $\frac{4}{3}\pi r^3$.)

b. Is the average density of the Sun (part a) more or less dense than water, which has a density of about **1000 kg/m³**?

c. The Sun is a gas. Do you think it is *more* or *less* dense than air? _____
   Explain your answer.

1. The greatest known snowfall was recorded in 1972 on Mt. Rainier in Washington, U.S.A. The snowfall measured 31.1 meters. How many feet of snow is this?

2. Is the following true? $\dfrac{\frac{a}{b}}{\frac{c}{d}} = \dfrac{a}{b}\left(\dfrac{c}{d}\right)^{-1}$ **?**

3. In the mnemonic for the order of operations *(Please Excuse My Dear Aunt Sally)*, the M stands for _____ and the D stands for _____.

4. Graph **x < 3** on the number line.

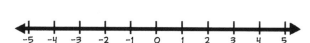

5. A bolt of lightning has a temperature of about 54,000° F. Change this temperature to Celsius.

Boom!

To do this, start by using the formula:
$F = \dfrac{9}{5}C + 32$.

Solve the equation for C and substitute to find the temperature in Celsius.

Crack!

Hisss

Celsius Temperature:

_____

1. The South Pole has no sunshine for 182 days of the year. What percent of the year is that?

2. Simplify: $\dfrac{6a^6 + 3a^6}{a^5}$

3. What property is shown? **(b − c)a = ba − ca**

- distributive property of multiplication over subtraction
- additive identity
- distributive property of multiplication over addition
- commutative property of multiplication

4. What is **y** when **x = 3** in the equation?
$$6 - 2x = y$$

5. A cumulus cloud about $\frac{1}{2}$ mile wide, $\frac{1}{2}$ mile long, and $\frac{1}{2}$ mile deep weighs about 1.5 billion pounds.

Density is equal to mass divided by volume.

$$\left(D = \dfrac{M}{V}\right)$$

What is the density of the cumulus cloud in pounds per cubic foot?

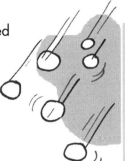

1. The biggest hailstones ever recorded fell in Bangladesh on the 14th of April, 1986. Each weighed over 1 kg. How many pounds did each hailstone weigh?

2. Rewrite the multiplication problem **8 • 64 = 512** using powers of two.

3. Is **4x** a factor of $4x^2 + 4x$?

4. Solve for **x**:   **6 + 4x = –6**
   Show all your work.

5. Several years ago, a tornado in Canada picked up a baby girl from her stroller and set her down miles away, unharmed and still asleep. Another tornado (this time in Connecticut) picked up a jar of pickles and dropped it a surprising distance away, unbroken.

The sum of the distances of these two events is 27 miles. The quantity *one less than three times the baby's distance*, when multiplied by five, equals the pickle distance. What are the distances?

What distance did . . .

the baby travel? ☐

the pickles travel? ☐

1. The wettest place on earth is Mawsynram, India. 11,873 mm of rain falls each year. How many feet of rain is this?

2.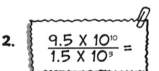
$$\frac{9.5 \times 10^{10}}{1.5 \times 10^{3}} =$$

3. Circle any value(s) the variable could **NOT** have in the following expression: $\dfrac{3}{2a}$

   1   π –1.5

   10^{10} 0 $\frac{1}{2}$ $\sqrt{2}$ 2^{-2}

4. Solve for **z**:

   1,000 + z + 3z + 3z = 9,400

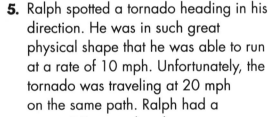

5. Ralph spotted a tornado heading in his direction. He was in such great physical shape that he was able to run at a rate of 10 mph. Unfortunately, the tornado was traveling at 20 mph on the same path. Ralph had a 15-minute head start.

How many minutes did it take for the tornado to catch Ralph?

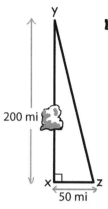

200 mi
50 mi

1. A pilot wants to fly around a storm front that is 25 miles wide and right in the center of her path from **x** to **y**. The distance from **x** to **y** is 200 miles. She flies 50 miles from **x** to **z** and then to **y**. How much farther does she fly than if she had been able to travel the straight line distance **x** to **y**?

2. Factor: $x^2 + 3x - 18$

3. Graph all the solutions for $3 \geq |x - 2|$ on the number line.

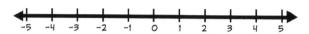

4. The sum of two numbers is 42. One of the numbers is **w**. Write an expression for the product of the numbers.

5. Challenge Problem

Los Angeles, California and Beirut, Lebanon both have a Mediterranean climate. The graph will help you find the information you need to answer the following questions about these two cities.

  a. On average, which city is wetter?

  b. Which function best describes the Mediterranean climate?

  ellipse   straight line   parabola   circle

  c. How many inches of rainfall are there in July in L.A. (on average)?

  d. How many inches of rainfall are there in November in Beirut (on average)?

  e. Between which two months in L.A. does the greatest decrease in rainfall occur?

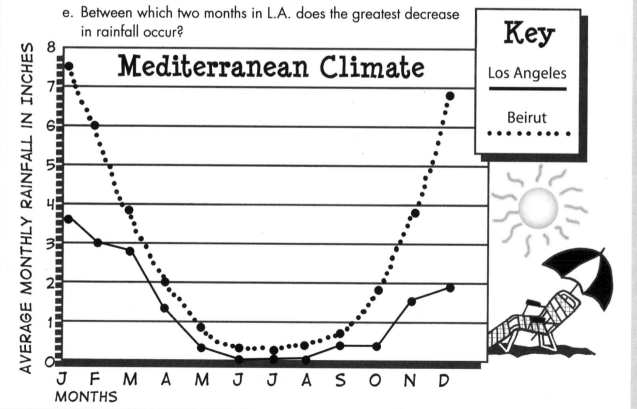

1. It seems people will go to great lengths to set unusual world records. A group of 9,234 students set the record for the longest human Domino line. The line stretched along a beach in Singapore for 2.6 miles.

   Approximately how much linear space was occupied by each student?

2. Square the quantity $(3a + b)$.

3. The union of two sets consists of

   _____

4. Write this equation in standard form:
   $$3y = -2x + 1$$

Pleenie L. Wingo
Longest Backward Walk

_____ miles

Ken Bannister
Most Banana-related Objects Collected

_____ objects

5. The larger of the two numbers in the records above is 1,000 more than two times the smaller number. Find the numbers if their difference is 9,000.

1. Rene Alvarenga has eaten more live scorpions than any other human being. He eats as many as 20 or 30 a day. Solve the equation to find out how many live scorpions Rene has eaten in his lifetime.

   $$x^2 = 1.225 \times 10^9$$

2. What is the slope of a line parallel to $y = mx + b$?

3. What is the prime factorization of 50?

4. Multiply: $(2x - y)(3x - y)$

5. Contestants throw rolling pins long distances in an effort to win the world record. Interestingly enough, it will take the same amount of time for a rolling pin that is tossed straight out to hit the ground as it takes for a rolling pin that is dropped to hit the ground. (They have the same vertical motion.)

   Assume a pin is projected straight out at a height of 6 ft. How long will it be in flight? (This is the same time it would take to drop!)

   USE THE FORMULA :

   $$h = -\tfrac{1}{2}gt^2 + h_0$$

   h is the height above ground at the end (in this case, zero), h_0 is the initial height, g is the acceleration due to gravity (32 ft/sec²), and t is time.

Name

1. K. S. Raghavendra set a unique record. He's the world's fastest egg crusher with the wrist. Find the number of eggs he crushed in 30 seconds by finding the value of **x** in the figure below. The perimeter of the rectangle is 156.

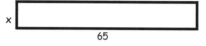

x | 65

2. Simplify:

$$\left(\frac{x^{-2}}{y^3}\right)^2$$

3. In an expression of the form **x^n**, **x** is called the _____

4. Solve for **y**: $3x + 2y = 4$

5. Jack decided to try to set a record for the world's largest guppy collection. He started by purchasing 8 guppies from Smart Pets, Inc. He figured that the guppy population would double every month. In a year, how many guppies will be in Jack's collection?

Guppy Tally:

Name

1. Solve for t:

$$d = \tfrac{1}{2} gt^2$$

2. Simplify:

$$\frac{x^3y^6z^2}{x^2y^3z}$$

3. What is the equation of a line with a **slope** equal to $-\frac{1}{2}$ and the **y-intercept** equal to **–6**?

4. Factor: $a^2 - 2ab + b^2$

Most Rattlesnakes Held in Mouth At One Time

Jackie Bibby held _____ rattlesnakes for **12.5** seconds.

Most Glasses Balanced on the Chin

Ashrita Furman balanced _____ twenty-oz glasses on his chin for **10.6** sec.

5. Two numbers are missing in the records above. Ten times the first number exceeds the second by five.

Represent the numbers by **n** and **7n + 19**. (*n = number of rattlesnakes*)

Find the numbers.

rattlesnakes

glasses

1. Write in symbols:

twenty-three less than the product of a number (w) and another number (k)

2. Factor: $a^2 + 2ab + b^2$

3. Does the parabola $y = x^2$ pass through the origin?

4. The correlation would be described as:

    a. little or none

    b. strong positive

    c. strong negative

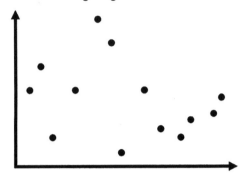

5. Challenge Problem

William "Snake" Hunter has 2,500 feet of snake-proof fencing. He will use it to fence in his rattlesnake collection, giving them at least 50,000 square feet in which to crawl around. The fourth side of his enclosure is a river. He decides not to fence along the river because he assumes that rattlesnakes can't swim (bad assumption!).

a. Write an expression for the length of the fence in terms of the width.

b. Write an expression for the area of the enclosure in terms of width.

c. Write a sentence expressing "Snake's" wish to give the rattlesnakes plenty of room.

_____

_____

_____

1. a. About how many times does this heart beat in a year?

b. If a person lives to be 72, about how many times does the heart beat in their lifetime?

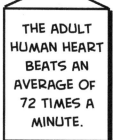

THE ADULT HUMAN HEART BEATS AN AVERAGE OF 72 TIMES A MINUTE.

2. Factor: $3x^2 + 5x - 12$

3. The money the bank pays you on the principal in an account is called _____.

4. Solve the following percent problems.

   a. **66** is **60%** of what number?

   b. **110%** of **200** is what number?

   c. What percent of **300** is **125**?

5. A CSI forensic pathologist wants to determine the height of a human victim from a crime scene. To do this, the scientist measures the length of the femur, then uses a formula to find the height. The formula used is $h = 69.089 + 2.238f$ where both the height (**h**) and the length of the femur (**f**) are in centimeters.

How tall in feet was the victim if the femur measured 51 cm?

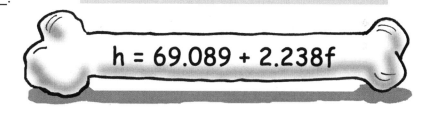

$h = 69.089 + 2.238f$

1. The small intestine has a length of 22 feet and a 2-inch circumference. Find its surface area in square feet.

2. Solve the equation:

$$(x - 9)^2 = 81$$

3. In the power x^n, **n** is the _____

4. Which is a solution for the equation?

$$y = \frac{3x}{2x + x}$$

   a. $y = x$

   b. $x = \frac{3}{2}$

   c. $x = -\frac{3}{2}$

   d. $y = \frac{3}{2x}$

5. About **80 ml** of blood moves into the lungs with each heart beat. An average resting heart rate is 72 beats per minute.

a. About how many liters of blood does the heart pump to the lungs in one year?

b. About how many gallons is this?

Explain how you solved the problem.

1. Joe has reduced his cholesterol level by 15% with diet and exercise. If his original level was 242, what is his cholesterol level now?

2. Solve the equation: 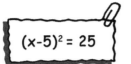 $(x-5)^2 = 25$

3. A polynomial with three terms is called

   _____

4. Find the area of the figure if its perimeter is 280 ft.

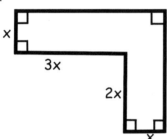

5. The normal stroke volume of the heart at rest is 80 ml. Alexis and Bob ran side by side on treadmills, both doing the same amount of work. Alexis's heart rate increased from 72 to 130 and his stroke volume increased to 100 ml. Bob's heart rate went from 72 to 150 and his stroke volume increased to 86 ml.

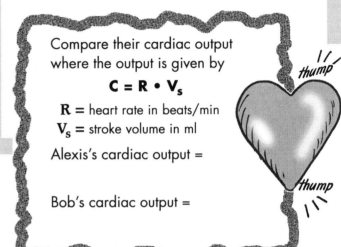

Compare their cardiac output where the output is given by

$$C = R \cdot V_s$$

R = heart rate in beats/min
V_s = stroke volume in ml

Alexis's cardiac output =

Bob's cardiac output =

thump
thump

1. The human brain has about 1×10^{11} brain cells. Once a person reaches the age of 35, he or she will start losing about 7,000 brain cells a day.
   a. How many cells would be lost by age 72?

   b. How many cells would be left by age 72?

2. One factor of $12x^2 + 24x$ is $12x$. The other factor must be (circle one):

   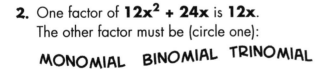
   MONOMIAL   BINOMIAL   TRINOMIAL

3. Define the multiplication property of zero.

4. Which is a solution for the equation?
   $$y = 3x^2 - 2x - 75 + 2x$$
   a. 5   b. 3   c. $\sqrt{10}$ d. –5

5. The body surface area (BSA) has a number of applications in medicine. It gives the surface area of the body in meters squared. One formula used to measure BSA is the Mosteller formula, named after the doctor who invented it. The formula is

   $$BSA = \sqrt{\frac{\text{height (in)} \cdot \text{weight (lb)}}{3131}}$$

   a. What is the BSA of a 6-ft, 180-lb person?

   b. Suppose that the person is ill and needs to take a powerful drug. The drug dose is 10 milligrams per meter squared (10 mg/m^2) of body surface area. How much drug will be administered in each dose to this person?

1. Simplify: $\dfrac{3y + 24}{-3}$

2. A cherry pie is cut into eight pieces. Each piece contains 15 grams of fat. Write an equation and solve it to find the total number of grams of fat in the pie.

3. Solve: $y = 6x^2 - 30x + 36$

(Hint: _It can be factored, but there are other ways to solve it. Use any way you choose._)

4. A sentence in which one or more variable(s) is put in terms of other variable(s) and number(s) is . . .

a. expression
b. formula
c. a null set
d. a counterexample

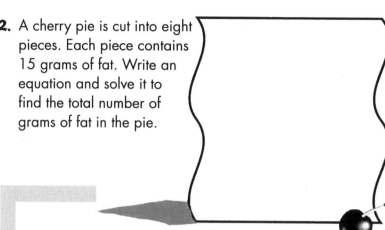

5. Challenge Problem

A young medical student taking an anatomy course has a box containing all the bones of an adult skeleton (206 bones). The number of bones in the adult human skeleton may be classified as shown on the box.

She takes a bone from the box at random in order to give herself an identification quiz. What is the probability that . . .

a. the bone comes from the upper extremity category?

b. it won't come from the upper extremity category?

c. it comes from the spine?

d. it comes from the face or the cranium?

e. if she draws two bones without replacing one of them, they will both come from the upper extremity category?

Write your probabilities in decimal form.

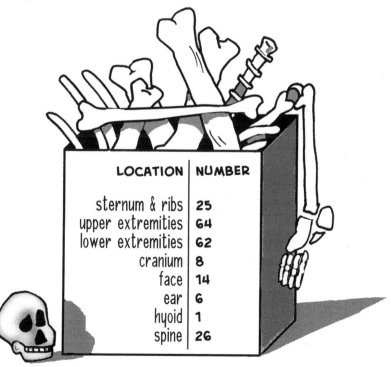

LOCATION	NUMBER
sternum & ribs	25
upper extremities	64
lower extremities	62
cranium	8
face	14
ear	6
hyoid	1
spine	26

1. At a salary of $22,500,000, Manny Ramirez (Boston Red Sox) was the highest paid U.S. baseball player in the U.S. in 2004.

   Write his salary in scientific notation.

2. Simplify: $\dfrac{x^2 - 3x - 10}{x^2 - 6x + 5}$

3. What is the equation of a line through the point **(−2, 3)** with a slope of **2**?

4. The sum of the goals scored by the two players equals 2,174. Twice Gretzky's goals minus Pele's goals equals 508. Find the number of career goals for each athlete.

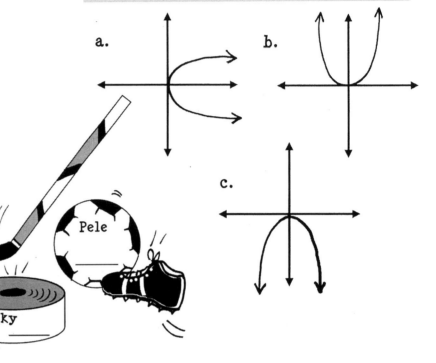

5. Which is a possible graph for **y = x²**?

   a.

   b.

   c.

1. Simplify the expression to find the average number of people at a Super Bowl party:

   $$\dfrac{6^2 \cdot 3^2 \cdot 18\sqrt{2}}{9 \cdot 36\sqrt{2}}$$

2. $\pm\sqrt{16} =$ _____

3. Is $(y + z)x$ the correct simplification for

   $y\sqrt{x} + z\sqrt{x}$?

4. Solve for **y**: $\sqrt{y + 3} = 6$

5. A top professional tennis player earned **x** dollars in competitions. He earned 175% that amount in endorsements of products. His total intake during his career was $80,850,000.

   a. Write an equation to find the amount he earned playing tennis.

   b. Write the solution.

   equation:

   solution:

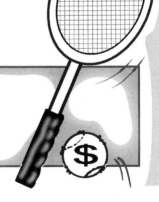

1. On average, 42,000 balls are used and 650 matches are played at the annual Wimbledon tennis tournament. At this rate, how many matches would have to be played to use 100,000 tennis balls? (*Round to the nearest whole number.*)

2. Simplify:

$$\frac{x^5 y^7}{x^{-2} y^4}$$

3. Is this solution correct? $\dfrac{4x + 2}{2} = 2x + 1$

4. Which is the correct graph? $x \geq -2$ **AND** $x \leq 4$

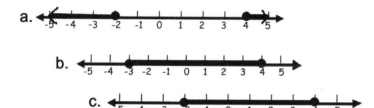

a.

b.

c.

5. Glenbrook South High School has 819 students. The girl-boy ratio in the school is 5:4. Twenty percent of the girls and twenty-five percent of the boys play sports. What percent (to the nearest tenth) of the school's student body participates in sports?

1. A famous bike racer puts a mixture of tea and sugar in his water bottle. He has a 2-gallon jug of 30% sugar tea and a 3-gallon jug of 20% sugar tea. What will be the percent of sugar if he mixes both jugs of tea together?

2. A regulation NBA basketball has a 9-inch diameter. What is its volume?

3. If **a > 0**, is the following true?

$$a^{\frac{1}{2}} \cdot a^{\frac{1}{2}} = \left(a^{\frac{1}{2}}\right)^2 = a^1 = a$$

4. The dimensions of home plate on a baseball field as usually given are shown here (slightly inaccurately):

a. The diagram implies that $12^2 + 12^2 = 17^2$ by what theorem?

b. Is the equation true?

5. This is a graph of

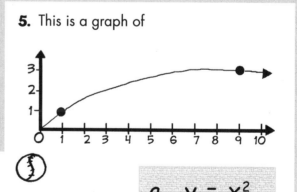

17 in

$8\frac{1}{2}$ in $8\frac{1}{2}$ in

12 in   12 in

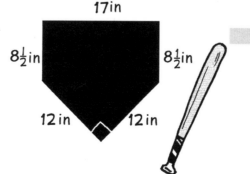

a. $y = x^2$

b. $y = -x^2$

c. $y = -\sqrt{x}$

d. $y = \sqrt{x}$

1. **a.** Use the formula to find the surface area of a basketball.

b. There are 122 "pebbles" per square inch on a Spalding basketball. How many pebbles are on the entire surface?

Surface Area of a Sphere

$$S = 4\pi r^2$$

d = 9 in

2. Solve for **x** *(beware of extraneous solutions!)*:

$$\sqrt{x + 6} = x$$

3. Find the product:

$$(2x + 4)(2x - 4)$$

4. Solve by factoring:

$$y = x^2 - 2x - 8$$

---

5. Challenge Problem

Largest NBA Arena	**Second largest NBA arena**	**Tenth largest NBA arena**
The Palace	United Center	Madison Square Garden
Auburn Hills, Michigan	Chicago, IL	New York, NY
home of the Detroit Pistons	home of the Chicago Bulls	home of the NY Knicks

- The Palace has 365 seats more than United Center.

- Madison Square Garden has 2,313 fewer seats than the Palace.

- The total seats in all three arenas is 63,550.

HOW MANY SEATS ARE IN EACH ARENA?

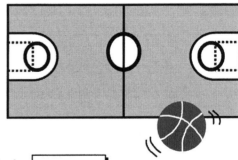

Number of seats in the **PALACE:**

Number of seats in **MADISON SQUARE GARDEN:**

Number of seats in the **UNITED CENTER:**

1. Solve the equation to find the number of cocoa beans needed to make a pound of chocolate.

$$y = 2x - 800$$

2. Factor: $6x^3y + 24x^2y + 12x^5y^2$

3. List four major subsets of the real numbers. Give an example of each.

4. What are the coordinates of the midpoint of a segment with these endpoints:

$A = (2, 3)$ and $B = (5, 5)$

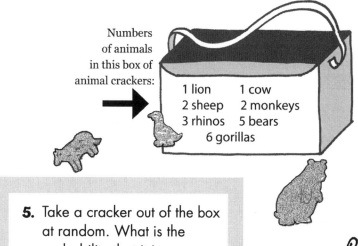

Numbers of animals in this box of animal crackers:

1 lion   1 cow
2 sheep   2 monkeys
3 rhinos   5 bears
       6 gorillas

5. Take a cracker out of the box at random. What is the probability that it is . . .
   a. a lion?
   b. not a cow?
   c. a donkey?
   d. a domestic animal?
   e. a gorilla or a rhino?

BONUS: TAKE TWO CRACKERS OUT OF THE BOX WITH REPLACEMENT. WHAT IS THE PROBABILITY THAT BOTH WILL BE BEARS?

1. A can of Spam is opened every **x** seconds somewhere on Earth. One in every **y** potatoes grown in the U.S. ends up in French fries.

Solve the system of equations to find **x** and **y**.

$$2x + y = 13$$
$$x + 3y = 19$$

2. Solve by factoring: $y = x^2 + x - 56$

3. a. What kind of equation is this?

$$\frac{10}{x} = \frac{7}{3}$$

   b. How do you solve it?
   c. What is the solution?

4. Given the points $A = (a, b)$ and $B = (c, d)$, write the formula to find the distance from A to B.

5. A confectioner wants to make a box to package his handmade chocolates. The material to make the box comes from a single square sheet of cardboard. The height of the box needs to be 2 inches and the volume of the box needs to be 128 in^3.

What is the necessary size for the original piece of cardboard?

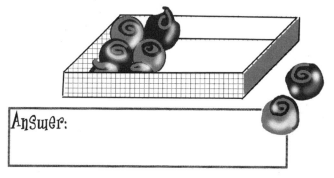

Answer:

1. Jimmy Dewar invented the Twinkie. It is said that he personally ate 40,177 of them in his lifetime. Is this number a prime number or a composite number?

2. Simplify: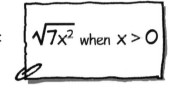
$\sqrt{7x^2}$ when $x > 0$

3. **3a + 2a = 5a** is an example of which property?
   a. multiplicative identity
   b. commutative property of addition
   c. additive identity
   d. distributive

4. What is the equation of a line with a slope of $-\frac{1}{3}$ through the point **(−1, −1)**?

5. An ice cream manufacturer has 7,500 gallons of a liquid that is $6\frac{2}{3}$% sugar. This is produced from a mixture of 2,500 gallons of liquid with 8% sugar and 5,000 gallons of liquid with an unknown sugar content.

Find the unknown percent of sugar in the second quantity of liquid.

Answer: _____ %

1. A recipe for a large batch of granola will taste the same (according to professional tasters) if the weight of the almond slices is within 2 pounds of 2,000 pounds.

Write an absolute value expression to express this "fact."

2. If the side of a square is $7\sqrt{7}$, what is the area of the square?

3. Which integers are **not** natural numbers?

4. Write an inequality for the set of numbers graphed below.

5. An ice cream cone is six inches in height with a radius of 1.5 inches at the top. (There is no ice cream in the cone.)

a. What is the volume of the cone?

b. Add a scoop of ice cream (a sphere with a radius of 1.5 inches). One-half of the scoop's volume is above the edge of the cone. What is the volume of the cone plus the ice cream that's above the edge?

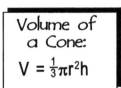
Volume of a Cone:
$V = \frac{1}{3}\pi r^2 h$

1.5 in

1. Find out how many cups of milk are needed to make one pound of butter by solving the equation for **x**:

$$2(x - 9) = 40$$

2. Which formula is easiest to use if you want to find **E**, given **m**, **g**, and **h**?

a. $m = \dfrac{E}{gh}$ c. $E = mgh$

b. $h = \dfrac{E}{mg}$ d. $g = \dfrac{E}{mh}$

3. Tell if each sentence is an equation or a formula.

4. Solve for C: **F = 32 + 1.8C**

Sentences	Equation (yes or no?)	Formula (yes or no?)
$A = \pi r^2$		
$2a > 0$		
$V = \frac{4}{3}\pi r^3$		
$|x - y| = 2$		

5. Challenge

Problem

At the Swirl-In Cafe, sixty-five percent of the customers order the super burger with fries. Seventy percent order the chocolate shake. If two out of five customers order both the burger and the shake, what is the probability that a customer has either the burger or the shake?

Answer: P = —————

SWIRL-IN CAFE
TODAY'S SPECIALS
SUPER BURGER WITH FRIES...$4.75
CHOCOLATE SHAKE.................$3.29

EXPLAIN HOW YOU SOLVED THE PROBLEM:

Burger...
Burger...
Burger...
Shake...
Shake...
Shake!

1. It is estimated that 300,000 people in the U.S. have climbed a rock wall. Falls are a risk of this sport, but fortunately, rock climbers have equipment to protect them from injury when they fall.

   You can find the time it takes a person to fall **32 feet** with the equation: $H = -16t^2$ (where H = *height above ground* and t = *time in seconds*.)

   Solve the equation for **t**.

2. What value *cannot* replace **z** in the expression?

   $$\frac{11}{9 - 3z}$$

3. Solve $y = x^2 - 10x + 23$ by completing the square.

4. Solve for **a**: $3a + 5a = 17a + 6b$

5. Which of the following proportions will give an answer to the problem below?

   a. $\dfrac{4.2}{1.4} = \dfrac{x}{6}$ c. $\dfrac{6}{1.4} = \dfrac{4.2}{x}$

   b. $\dfrac{4.2}{1.4} = \dfrac{6}{x}$ d. $\dfrac{4.2}{6} = \dfrac{x}{1.4}$

In the U.S., about 4.2 million high school students participated in sports during the 2005–2006 academic year. An estimated 1.4 million sports-related injuries occurred among these students. At this rate, how many injuries would be expected to occur if there were 6 million students involved in high school sports?

Answer:

OUCH!

1. Staff members at a local hospital noticed a sharp increase in orthopedic injuries from 2005 to 2006. In 2005, the emergency room treated 740 patients with orthopedic injuries. In 2006, the number climbed to 990.

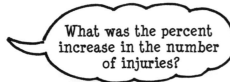

What was the percent increase in the number of injuries?

2. Simplify: $\sqrt{18} + \sqrt{50}$

3. Is this statement true or false?

   The absolute value of every number is positive.

4. Write an algebraic equation for the value of **x** quarters, **y** dimes, and **z** nickels.

5. At Bruno's Gym, the staff has been working to reduce the number of injuries among their boxing students. Three years ago, they had 180 injuries in the year. Their goal was to reduce that number by 10. Bruno is happy to report that since then, they have kept the rate within ten of that goal for each year.

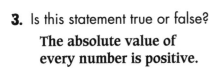

a. Draw a graph on the number line to represent the new number of injuries. (Label the graph.)

b. Write an absolute value equation to describe the boundaries; give its solution.

1. In a study of high school sports injuries, the overall injury rate for football was 4.36 per 1,000. This means that a high school football player who participates in 1,000 games and practices can expect 4.36 injuries.

At this rate, how many injuries would be expected in a high school with 100 football players whose practices and games total 200?

2. Solve: $y = x^2 + 6x - 16$

3. Jack tosses a penny twice.

a. How many combinations of heads and tails can he get? List them.

b. How many permutations can he get? List them.

4. Solve the system by graphing.

$y = x + 2$
$y = -x - 4$

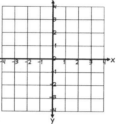

5. A nurse has two liters of a 30% alcohol solution. He wants to use a 15% solution to disinfect a hockey injury. How much of a 10% alcohol solution will the nurse have to add to the 30% solution to dilute it to 15%?

Answer: _____

1. Each year in the U.S, there are 50,000 visits to hospital emergency rooms as a result of skateboarding injuries. 1,500 of the injured skateboarders are hospitalized.

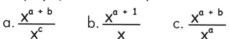

What percentage of skateboarding injuries result in hospitalization?

2. Simplify: *(Assume x > 0)*

a. $\dfrac{x^{a+b}}{x^c}$ b. $\dfrac{x^{a+1}}{x}$ c. $\dfrac{x^{a+b}}{x^a}$

3. Find the ratio of the volume of a sphere to its surface area.

4. Arrange the numbers in descending order:

4.55×10^{-2} $\sqrt{.02}$ $.067$

$.05321$ $\dfrac{9}{100}$

5. An ambulance traveled to pick up an injured snowboarder at the ski hill and returned to the hospital. The total travel time was two hours. Of that, 15 minutes was spent getting the injured person ready for transport. The average rate going out was 40 mph and the average rate returning to the hospital was 30 mph.

a. How long did it take in each direction?

b. How far was the ski hill from the hospital?

DAREDEVIL'S DROP BEWARE!

1. In 2004, there were 89,000 emergency room visits with trampoline injuries from home trampolines. Fifteen percent of these injuries were to children under the age of six. How many children under six went to the emergency room with trampoline injuries?

3. Write a formula for the area of a triangle that is half of a square with sides **x**.

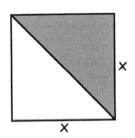

2. What is the distance between the points?

   A = (–4, 6) and **B (–2, 10)**

4. If x + 6 = 10, find the value of the expression:
$$2(x + 6)^2 - x + \frac{6}{2}$$

5. Challenge Problem

Suppose an original colony of 2,000 bacteria (which doubles every hour) escapes at 10 a.m.

a. How many bacteria will there be at noon? _____ at 4:00 p.m.? _____

b. Surgery is the only way to treat this infection, because of its location. In your opinion, should surgery be scheduled for today or tomorrow?

Dear Aunt Peg,

Thanks for the get-well card. I'm feeling much better now. I was lucky to escape alive from the fire. I had to spend some time in the hospital because of smoke inhalation.

The doctor said that fast-growing bacteria from an infection in my lungs was about to wreak havoc in my body. A colony of bacteria escaped from my pleural cavity and began multiplying like crazy! Antibiotics were useless because there was no blood supply to carry them to the location of the bacteria between the tissues.

The doctor performed surgery just in time, and now I'm on the mend.

      Your loving niece,
      Emily

1. A flea jumped from A to B (which is a true distance a flea can jump). Find the distance.

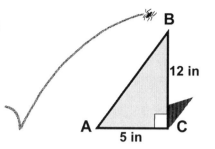

B

12 in

A   5 in   C

2. Solve for **r**: $V = \pi r^2 h$

3. Find the equation of the line perpendicular to $y = 2x + 3$ through the point **(1, 5)**.

4. Write the **quadratic formula**.

5. Sam's pet jumping spider, Sophia, can jump **x** inches high and **y** inches long. Solve the system of equations to find the distances that she can jump.

$$2x + y = 27$$
$$3x - 2y = -5$$

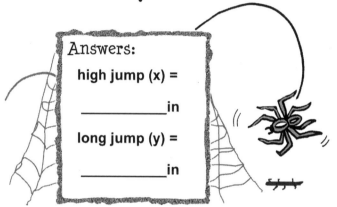

Answers:

high jump (x) =

_____ in

long jump (y) =

_____ in

1. A group of people decided to try for a world jumproping record. They all jumped over the same rope at the same time. Their effort was a success. To find out how many people were in this group, solve the following equation:

$$\frac{14x^2}{7x} - 50 = 390$$

2. Simplify:

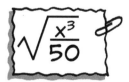

$$\sqrt{\frac{x^3}{50}}$$

3. Give the slope of a line parallel to:

$$2y + 3x = 6$$

4. Solve: $2\sqrt{x - 8} = -3$

5. A flea, when jumping, accelerates **n** times faster than a space shuttle.

If a number is **squared** and then **decreased** by forty times the original number, the result is 500.

Take the positive root of this equation to find out how fast the flea accelerates in relationship to the shuttle.

Beware the extraneous root!

1. A red kangaroo can cover great distances in one bound and can leap far off the ground. Find the tangent of angle A to learn how high (in ft) the red kangaroo can jump.

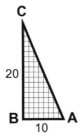

2. The graph of $y = ax^2$ is a parabola.

a. What are the coordinates of its vertex?

b. Is it symmetric to the x-axis or the y-axis?

c. What are the conditions on **a** that tell whether the parabola opens up or down?

3. Solve by factoring: $2x^2 + 5x = 12$

4. Simplify: $\dfrac{\sqrt{x^7} - \sqrt{x^5}}{\sqrt{x^3}}$

5. Freddy has an unusual ailment for a frog. He is afraid of water. Freddy wants to get across the river, so he plans to jump from rock to rock (thus avoiding the water). The rocks have numbers on them. The product of the numbers on the rocks that Freddy uses is 23,205. (He does not hop on any rock more than once.) What are the rocks Freddy lands on?

1. A jerboa (desert rat) can jump many times its body length. To find the distance a jerboa could jump, determine the number that is the measure of angle A in the triangle described.

- It is a right triangle.
- Its sides are 1 and 1.
- The hypotenuse is $\sqrt{2}$.
- Angle A is not the right angle.

2. Simplify: $\sqrt{2} + \sqrt{32}$

3. Is the statement below true or false?

The solution to any quadratic equation can be found by using the quadratic formula.

4. Solve for **a**: $a^2 + b^2 = c^2$

5. Charlie Cricket tries to jump across a room to meet a prospective girlfriend, Carmella. The distance is five feet. Charlie is able to jump a foot forward at a time. However, due to his excessive shyness, Charlie jumps backwards every other jump. These backwards jumps are one-half foot in distance.

a. Does Charlie ever meet Carmella?

b. If so, how many jumps does it take?

1. Fleas are the longest jumpers of any animal in the world. A flea can jump 150 times its body length. If a certain flea can jump thirteen inches, how long is its body?

2. When two triangles are similar, corresponding angles are _____ and corresponding sides are _____.

3. Find the general term for the geometric sequence:

3, 5, 9, 17, 33, . . .

4. Solve **y = x² – 2x – 10** by using the quadratic formula.

Show your work.

5. Challenge Problem

The vertical displacement is given by
$$h = \frac{1}{2}gt^2$$

h = height above the water
g = acceleration of gravity = 32 ft/sec²
t = time

The horizontal displacement is given by
$$x = vt$$

x = horizontal distance
v = horizontal velocity
t = time

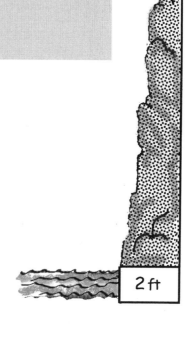

2 ft

Use the information on the diagram and the formulas to solve the problems.

A grasshopper that is able to run one meter per second launches himself horizontally at 1m/sec off a cliff 144 feet high toward the sea below.

    a. How long will it take the grasshopper to reach the water?

    b. When he lands, how far will he have traveled horizontally?

    c. Will he land in the water?

1. In 1980, Mt. St. Helens exploded with a force so powerful that it sent ash spewing out over an area of 212 square miles.

Assuming that the volcano spread its ash in a circle with the volcano at the center, what is the radius of the area covered by ash?

2. Give the fifth term of the geometric series: $2^n + 3$ (where *n* represents the term).

3. Define:
  a. the range of a function
  b. the domain of a function

4. Write the equation of a line through the points **A = (5, −1)** and **B = (−3, 3)**.

5. At −273°C, all the heat energy would be removed from a gas. It is impossible to reduce the temperature further. This temperature is called *absolute zero*. There is a temperature scale based on absolute zero named after a British physicist, Lord Kelvin.

The formula for converting Celsius to Kelvin
$$K = C + 273^0$$

The formula for converting Kelvin to Fahrenheit
$$F = \frac{9}{5}K - 460^0$$

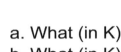

a. What (in K) is **0°C**?
b. What (in K) is **−10°C**?
c. What (in K) is **10°C**?
d. What is absolute zero in Fahrenheit?

1. The Great Fire of San Francisco (which followed an earthquake in 1906) destroyed 12 square kilometers of the city. Find this area in square miles.

2. Express $\sqrt{\dfrac{50}{32}}$ as the ratio of two integers.

3. What is the range of this function?
$$f(x) = 3 + \sqrt{x}$$

4. Use the graph of the line to determine its slope.

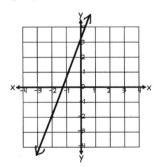

$$Q = mC\Delta T$$

Q = the heat lost or gained (in Joules)

m = mass (in kilograms)

C = the specific heat (the amount of energy, measured in Joules, that it takes to heat one kilogram of a substance one degree Celsius)

ΔT = change in temperature (in Celsius)

5. The specific heat of water is very high. That is why water is used to take away the heat from a car engine. The measurement of the specific heat of water is 4,180 Joules per kilogram (J/kg). How much heat is absorbed by 3×10^2 kg of water when it is heated from 10°C to 80°C?

1. The temperature on the Sun is 9932°F. Write this temperature in Celsius.

2. Let **f(x) = |x + 1|**. Then calculate:

   f(2)   f(0)   f(–1)   f($-\frac{3}{4}$)

3. a. Solve **y = 3x² + 4x – 5** by using the quadratic formula.

   b. What are the values for **a**, **b**, and **c** in the quadratic equation for this problem?

4. Solve by graphing:
   y = x² – 5x + 4

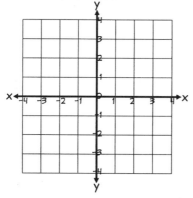

5. The hottest temperature on Earth is represented by **x**. The coldest is represented by **y**. These measurements are in Fahrenheit.

Solve the system to find these temperatures.

2x + y = 143.4°
x – 2y = 393.2°

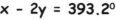

1. The Tunguska Blast (thought to be caused by an exploding asteroid) occurred in a remote region of Siberia in 1908. The force of the blast was equal to 20 million tons of exploding TNT. The atomic bomb dropped at Hiroshima in 1945 was equal to 20,000 tons of TNT. How much bigger (in percent) was the Tunguska Blast than the bomb?

2. Evaluate for **a = 3, b = 1, c = 0**.

   a. **(2bᶜ)ᵃ**   b. **aᵇ**   c. **(2ᵃ – 3b)ᶜ**

3. When two triangles are **congruent**, corresponding angles are _____ and corresponding sides are _____.

4. What would you add to the expression below to make it a perfect trinomial?

   x² + 14x +____

A basalt lava flow in a channel on a steep slope can travel faster than 19 miles per hour.

5. Suppose that a particular volcano is a symmetric cone with a base circumference of 50 miles and a height of 2 miles. How long will it take for lava to travel in a channel straight down from the top of the mountain to the base?

1. a. Graph **y < 4** on the number line.

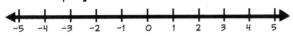

b. Graph **y < 3** on the coordinate grid.

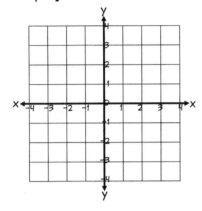

2. What is the domain of the function with the rule?

$$f(x) = \frac{x + 1}{x - 1}$$

The domain is:
_____

3. The total heat produced in one day by the human body would light a 60-watt light bulb for $1\frac{1}{2}$ days. (A watt is a measure of power.)

a. Assuming a constant rate, how many light bulbs could you light up in a lifetime of 72 years?

b. How many watts are produced in the 72 years?

4. Factor: **$12a^2 + 25a + 12$**

5. Challenge Problem

The total energy given off by the Sun (one big nuclear explosion) is **1.2×10^{24} Joules** per year.

3.8×10^9 Joules (of energy) are given off when one ton of TNT explodes.

According to some official estimates, the nuclear bomb used at Hiroshima was equivalent in energy to the explosion of 20,000 tons of TNT.

Use the information above to solve the problems.

a. The energy given off by the Sun in one year is equivalent to _____ tons of TNT.

b. This amount of energy given off by the Sun in one year is equivalent to _____ Hiroshima-sized bombs.

MONDAY WEEK 33 _____ MATH PRACTICE
Name

1. Avid tiddlywinks players compete to see who can flip the most of the round plastic chips into a pot. The world champion flipped 10,000 tiddlywinks into a pot in about 3 hr, 52 min. At the same rate, how long would it take to flip 3,500 tiddlywinks into a pot?

2. Simplify: a. $\dfrac{w^7}{w^3}$ c. $w^4 \cdot w^3 \cdot w$

   b. $\left(\dfrac{w^2}{w^3}\right)^{\frac{1}{2}}$ d. $\left(\dfrac{2w^2}{3}\right)^3$

3. Find **tan A** = _____

   a. $\dfrac{c}{a}$ b. $\dfrac{b}{c}$ c. $\dfrac{a}{b}$ d. $\dfrac{b}{a}$

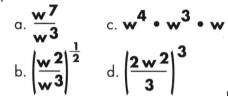

4. Solve by factoring:

   $y = x^2 - 7x + 10$

5. A newspaper will typically pay $300 to someone who creates a Sunday crossword puzzle and $75 for a weekday crossword.

Mia made $45,000 creating crossword puzzles last year. If she created four times as many weekday puzzles as she did Sunday puzzles, how many of each kind did she create?

Weekday Tally: Sunday Tally:

TUESDAY WEEK 33 _____ MATH PRACTICE
Name

1. The world's largest jigsaw puzzle has 21,600 pieces and an area of 58,435 square feet. On average, what is the size of each piece (in square inches)?

2. Simplify: $\dfrac{28a^2 - 35a + 14}{14}$

3. If **n** is an integer, can $n^2 + n$ be written as the product of two consecutive integers?

4. Find the area of triangle ABC.

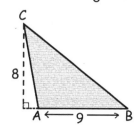

5. A record was set on a miniature golf course by a golfer who played **w** holes in **x** hours. He played the **y**-foot course **z** times to do this.

Solve the following system to find w, x, y, and z.

$w + x = 3059$
$x + y = 1121$
$x + z = 193$
$z + y + w = 4301$

©Incentive Publications, Inc., Nashville, TN   **101**   Use It! Don't Lose It! IP 613-4

1. Some avid puzzle-makers set a record for the jigsaw puzzle with the most pieces. The puzzle had 212,323 pieces and measurements of 35.5-foot width and 38.25-foot length.

What is the average size of a puzzle piece (in square inches)?

2. Simplify:
$$3(x^2 + 2x) - 2x^2$$

3. What is the equation for . . .

the x-axis? _____ the y-axis? _____

4. Graph **x ≥ −2** on the coordinate plane.

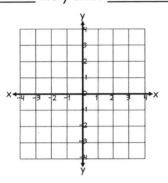

5. As a contestant on a game show, you are offered your choice of three doors. Behind each door is a prize: a donkey, a Cadillac, or another donkey. You really want a donkey!

a. You select a door. Before it is opened, the game show host opens one of the doors you did not choose, and you see a donkey. You are offered a chance to switch doors. If you don't switch, what is your probability of getting the donkey?

b. If you do switch to an unopened door, what is the probability of your getting your heart's desire?

1. The world's largest yo-yo has a circumference of 389.36 inches. What is its radius?

2. Simplify: $\dfrac{3}{2x} + \dfrac{6z}{2x}$

3. Find **sin A =**

4. Given these equations,

$$|a| = 0 \qquad |a| = -1 \qquad |a| = 1$$

a. Which has one solution?

b. Which has no solution?

c. Which has two solutions?

5. Complete the table and graph for
$$y = -x - 1.$$

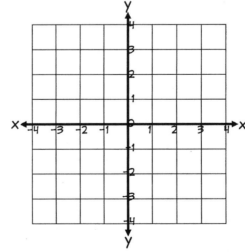

X	Y
−1	
0	
1	
2	

1. Mathias Aesch, from Germany, holds the world record for stacking Dominoes. He stacked 726 of them on a single vertical standing Domino.

   a. Suppose a Domino is **1 x 2 x $\frac{1}{4}$** inches. What is the volume of Mathias's stack?

   b. Does the way he stacks them affect the volume?

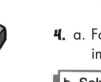

2. Find the value of **x** in the triangle.

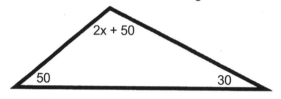

2x + 50

50   30

3. Write **x + 5y = 10** in the slope-intercept form.

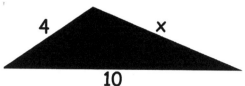

4   x

10

4. a. For the triangle above, write three inequalities that involve **x**.

   b. Solve the inequalities for x.

   c. **x** must be greater than _____

   d. **x** must be less than _____

5. Challenge Problem

Here is a table showing all the possible outcomes when a pair of dice is thrown.

a. The total number of outcomes = _____

b. If the first die is 3, what is the probability that the sum is greater than six?_____

c. If the first die is a 5, what is the probability that the sum is ≥ 8?_____

d. If the first die is a 6, what is the probability that the sum is 7?_____

Die 1	Die 2	Die 1 + Die 2	Die 1	Die 2	Die 1 + Die 2
1	1	2	4	1	5
1	2	3	4	2	6
1	3	4	4	3	7
1	4	5	4	4	8
1	5	6	4	5	9
1	6	7	4	6	10
2	1	3	5	1	6
2	2	4	5	2	7
2	3	5	5	3	8
2	4	6	5	4	9
2	5	7	5	5	10
2	6	8	5	6	11
3	1	4	6	1	7
3	2	5	6	2	8
3	3	6	6	3	9
3	4	7	6	4	10
3	5	8	6	5	11
3	6	9	6	6	12

1. Represent the age of each person algebraically.
   a. The sum of Bill's age (b) and Rob's age (r) is 30.
   b. Anna (a) is 12 years older than Carl (c).
   c. Laura's present age is x. What will her age be in six years?
   d. Ezzie's age x years ago (if her present age is 15).

2. Is the following statement true or false?

   If y varies directly as x, then y = kx where k is called a constant of variation.

3. Simplify (rationalize the denominator): $\sqrt{\dfrac{4}{3}}$

4. Susan is three times as old as Blake is now. In fifteen years, she will be ten years older than Blake. How old are they now?

5. Graph $y = -x^2$ and $y = x^2$ on the same set of axes.

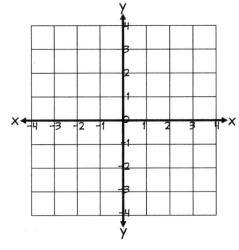

SUSAN   BLAKE

1. Jordy Lemoine of France is the youngest known solo rap artist. To determine the age of this talented kid, find the positive root of the quadratic equation:

$$(x + 2.5)^2 = 49$$

2. By what number would you multiply $\dfrac{3}{\sqrt{5}}$ to rationalize the denominator?

3. Find **cos A = _____**

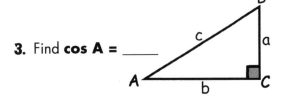

4. If **y** varies directly as **x** and **y = 8** when **x = 2**, find **y** if **x = 4**.

5. A radioactive isotope of Carbon, called Carbon 14, decays exponentially with a half-life of 5,730 years. The formula below can be used to find the age of Carbon 14.

   An original sample of two grams of Carbon 14 would be only one gram after the passage of 5,730 years.

   How old (now) is an original sample of 100 grams if it weighs . . .

   a. 50 grams?
   b. 25 grams?
   c. 12.5 grams?
   d. 6.25 grams?

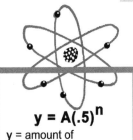

$$y = A(.5)^n$$

y = amount of Carbon 14 remaining
A = original amount of Carbon 14 in sample
n = number of 5,730-year intervals

1. Let **x** represent the age of "Banana" George Blair, the oldest barefoot skier in the world. Let **y** represent the age of Little Peggy March, the world's youngest female singer to have a # 1 top hit. Solve the following system to find their ages:

$$x + y = 102$$
$$x - y = 72$$

2. Simplify: $\left(x^{\frac{1}{3}}\right)^4 \bullet \left(x^5\right)^{\frac{1}{3}}$

3. Is this statement true or false?

If y varies inversely as x, then xy = k where k is a constant of variation.

4. In triangle ABC,
a = _____
and c = _____

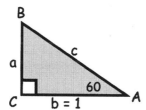

5. In medieval France, two aging monks left their home monastery and traveled in opposite direction. One monk traveled two miles a day further than the other. At the end of thirty days, they are 360 miles apart. Find the speed at which each monk traveled.

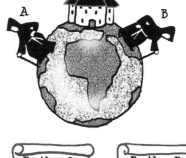

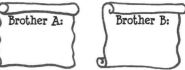

Brother A: Brother B:

1. What are the two equations you would use to solve the following age problem?

John (j) is six times Sally's age (s). Two years from now, John will be ten times as old as Sally was three years ago. How old are they now?

2.
a. Does $\sqrt{a + b} = \sqrt{a} + \sqrt{b}$?
b. Does $\sqrt{a \bullet b} = \sqrt{a} \bullet \sqrt{b}$?

3. Assume **y** varies inversely as **x**, and **y = 8** when **x = 2**. Write an equation to show how **x** and **y** are related.

4. Simplify: $\left(x^{\frac{1}{2}}\right)^5$

5. The sum of Sara's and Krista's ages is 25. In 12 years, Sara will be seven years older than four times as old as Krista was five years ago.

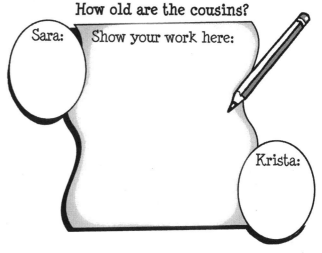

How old are the cousins?

Sara: Show your work here:

Krista:

1. The oldest living human being on record died in France in August of 1997. The positive root of the following quadratic equation yields a number that was her age:

$$(x + 3)^2 = 15,625$$

What year was she born?

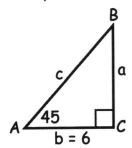

B
c
a
A 45
b = 6
C

```
┌─────────────────────┐
│ 2. Find c and a     │
│    in the triangle. │
│                     │
│  a = _____  │
│                     │
│  b = _____  │
└─────────────────────┘
```

3. Factor: $6a^2 - 8a - 30$

4. Write T (true) or F (false) for each sentence:

a. $\sqrt[3]{a^2} = a^{\frac{2}{3}}$

b. $\sqrt[6]{a^3} = a^{\frac{1}{2}}$

c. $\sqrt[7]{a^2} = a^{\frac{7}{2}}$

5. Challenge Problem

Fill in the missing numbers. *(x = the same number in all cases)*

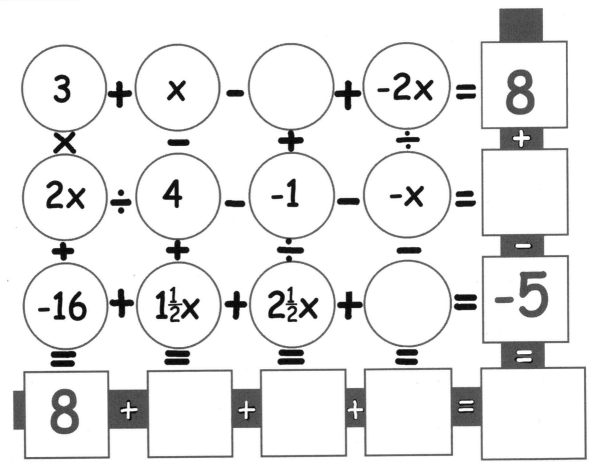

MONDAY WEEK 35 _____ MATH PRACTICE
Name

1. How much interest is earned in ten years on $1,000 principal at a rate of 5% annually?

2. Give the domain and range of the function:
   { (3, 4), (4, 3), (5, 2), (6, 3) }

3. What is the slope and x-intercept of the line **2x + 3y = 9**?

4. Find the length of the hypotenuse (x).

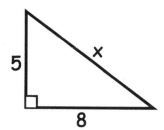

5. A Subaru that cost $28,000 new in 2000 began depreciating in value *exponentially*. It depreciated 35% over the first 7 years.

What is its value in . . .

a. 2007?_____

b. 2014?_____

TUESDAY WEEK 35 _____ MATH PRACTICE
Name

1. Scott paid $6.50 for lunch and had less than $20 in his wallet after that. Write and solve an inequality that represents the amount of money Scott could have had in his wallet before lunch.

2. Which is a function?

   a. 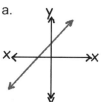   b.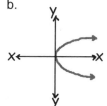

3. Write the equation in standard form:
   $$\frac{1}{2}x + \frac{1}{4}y = 1$$

4. Solve and graph the inequality.
   −2x + 6 ≤ 10 _____

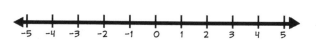

5. The Swirl-In is having a promotion; they are giving away free food. There is a sack with two thousand coupons. Seven hundred are coupons for a free burger. One thousand coupons are for a free shake, and three hundred are for free fries.

a. One coupon is drawn. What is the probability of getting a free shake?

b. Two coupons are drawn (with replacement). What is the probability of getting a burger AND fries?

c. Two coupons are drawn (with replacement). What is the probability of getting a burger OR fries?

1. A store sells hats with a profit of $6.00 a hat. How many hats must the store sell to make a profit of at least $50,000?

2. Simplify: **a.** $\dfrac{a^c}{a^d}$ **b.** $\dfrac{z^{m+1}}{z}$

3. Given: **y** varies directly as **x**. When **y** is 16, **x** is 4. What will **y** be when **x** is 6?

4. Solve for **x**:

$$3x - 5 = 2x + 16$$

5. Bill and Sally both have new lawn mowers. They want to start a business mowing lawns together in the summer. Sally's lawn mower is bigger than Bill's. With his mower, Bill can mow six lawns in eight hours, while Sally is able to mow seven lawns in five hours.

How long will it take them to mow a dozen lawns together?

Bill Mows Better! 555-7707

MOW YOUR LAWN (FAST) CALL SALLY 555-1212 (GOT A NEW MOWER!)

1. Solve: $|x - 3| < 7$

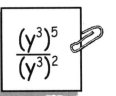

2. Aaron lives in a state where the sales tax is 6%. He wants to buy an SUV and donate it to a local children's camp. The SUV's marked price is $35,000. What is the total Aaron must pay?

3. Simplify: $\dfrac{(y^3)^5}{(y^3)^2}$

4. Give the domain and range of each function:
a. $f(x) = 2x + 5$
b. $f(x) = (x - 3)^2$

5. Insurance companies may use a quadratic equation to model the relationship between the age of drivers and the number of accidents.

Here is an example:
$$y = .4x^2 - 36.8x + 1036.4$$

where **y** = the number of accidents per 50 million miles driven and **x** = the age of the driver.

a. Based on the model, who is less likely to have an accident, a 16-year old driver or a 72-year old driver?
b. How many accidents does the model predict for a 40-year old driver?
c. If you have a graphing calculator, find the minimum for the model.

1. The library in the town of Sparta has a goal of providing six books for every eleven persons living in the town. The population of Sparta is 13,543. Currently, the library has 3,500 books. How many more books do they need to buy to reach their goal?

2. Simplify:

$$3\sqrt{2} - \sqrt{5} + 6\sqrt{2} + 9\sqrt{5}$$

3. Solve: $3x^2 = 432$

    a. 12   **c.** 72

    b. ±12   **d.** ±72

4. How tall is the stack of books?

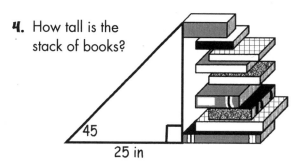

45

25 in

5. Challenge Problem

The graph of a system of inequalities on a coordinate plane can result in a polygon. Below is a polygon that satisfies four inequalities.

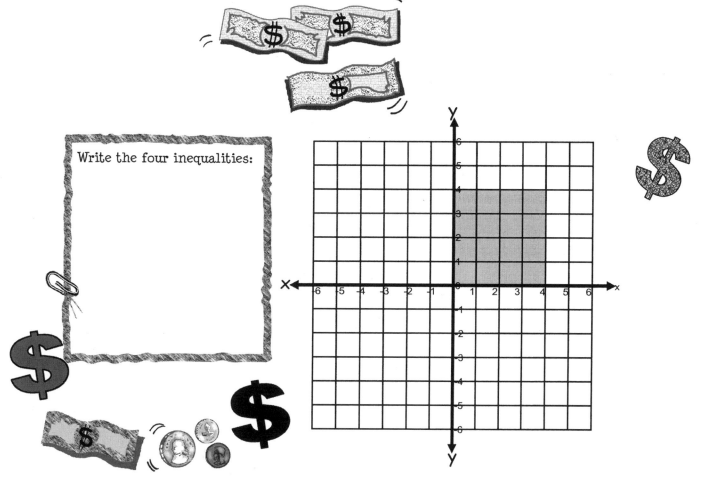

Write the four inequalities:

1. Colorado Jones has fallen into a hole 30 feet deep. The sides of the hole are very slippery. Every day, he can only climb up three feet, but for each for each three feet he climbs, he slips back two. Does Colorado ever get out of the hole? If so, how many days does it take?

2. What is the domain and the range of the following exponential function: $y = 2^x$?

3. Expand and simplify:

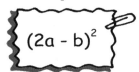
$$(2a - b)^2$$

4. a. Write **2x + 2y = 5** in slope-intercept form.

   b. What is the slope?

      c. What is the y-intercept?

5. Use Hooke's Law to determine the force constant of a spring, which is stretched **.75 meters** by a force of 25 Newtons.

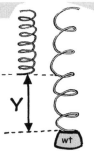

A Newton is equivalent to the weight of an average apple. (This is easy to remember if you know the story of Newton and the apple.)

Hooke's Law illustrates direct variation. The formula for the law is **F= KY** where
F = force (in Newtons) that stretches a spring
Y = the distance the spring stretches (in meters)
K = the "force constant" of the spring

1. A laser printer can print 15 pages a minute. A science teacher wants to print the manual for "How To Use A Telescope" for each of his 500 students. The manual is four pages long. How long will it take the printer to do this job?

2. a. The graph of **y = |x| + 2** looks like . . .

   O a triangle   O an angle   O a parabola

   b. What is its vertex?

3. What property justifies $\left(\dfrac{x}{y}\right)^n = \dfrac{x^n}{y^n}$

4. Graph all solutions to **|x − 0| > 2**.

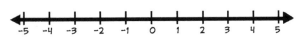

5. At 10 a.m., a Corvette leaves Ashland, Oregon, traveling north on Interstate #5. At the same time, a Porsche leaves Portland, Oregon, traveling south on the same highway. The Corvette averages 65 miles per hour. The Porsche averages 75 miles per hour. The distance between Ashland and Portland is 300 miles.

a. When will the cars meet?

b. How far will each car have traveled?

1. Which are linear equations?

    a. y = mx + b   **c. y = |x|**

    b. y = x²   **d. y = kx**

2. The Natural Gas Law relates pressure, volume, and temperature of a gas to the number of atoms in the gas. The formula for the Natural Gas Law is **PV = nRT**.

    Solve this equation for n.

3. Solve: **x² + 6x + 9 = 144**

4. a. Area of the circle = _____

    b. Area of the square = _____

    c. Area of the shaded region = _____

5. A chemist has 100 liters of an acid solution that contains 18 liters of pure acid. How many liters of acid must be added to make a 40% acid solution?

Answer: _____

1. Georgia has made a lemonade mixture that is 30% pure lemon juice and 70% water. She sells a 9-ounce glass at her lemonade stand.

    a. How much pure lemon juice is in that glass?

    b. How much water is in a **y**-ounce glass of the same mixture?

2. Give the property that justifies the step.

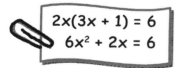

$$2x(3x + 1) = 6$$
$$6x^2 + 2x = 6$$

3. Sam thinks $(x^3)^4 = x^7$. Is he right?

4. Ted, Fred, and Ned each run 100-yard dash at a uniform speed. Ted beats Fred by 10 yards and Fred beats Ned by 10 yards.

    By how much does Ted beat Ned?

5. Graph the solution to the system:

    $y \leq |x|$ $y \geq 0$ $x \geq 0$

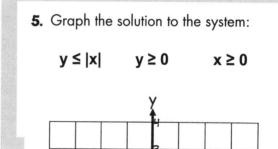

1. The amount of heat lost through a glass window is given by

$$H = KA(T_i - T_o)$$

Solve the equation for T_o.

2. Factor:

$$x^2 - y^2w^2$$

3. Find the slope of a line parallel to:

$$y = mx + b$$

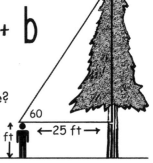

4. How tall is the tree?

60

5 ft   ←25 ft→

5. Challenge Problem
Teetering in the Balance

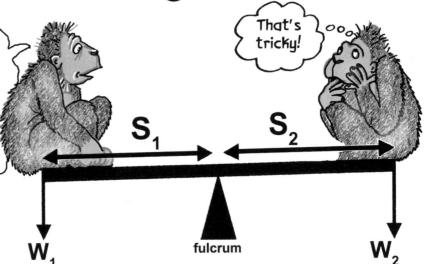

S_1 S_2

W_1 fulcrum W_2

Hint: The condition for the teeter-totter to balance is $S_1 \cdot W_1 = S_2 \cdot W_2$ where S_1 and S_2 are the distances from the fulcrum, and W_1 and W_2 are weights on each end of the teeter-totter.

Speech bubble: Hey, Gonzo, can you answer this question? If you weigh **120 pounds** and sit **6 feet** from the fulcrum, and I weigh **130 pounds** . . . how far from the fulcrum do *I* need to sit in order to balance you?

Speech bubble: That's tricky!

a. Answer the gorilla's question (above).

b. Fill in the table by calculating the weights that would be needed to balance 100 pounds (W_1) at 5 feet from the fulcrum (S_1).

c. $S_2 \cdot W_2$ is a constant. What is the constant in this case (in item **b** above)? *Round to the nearest whole number.*

d. Circle the correct answer: *When two variables multiplied together equal a constant, the variation is (direct, inverse).*

S_2 (ft)	W_2 (lbs)
1	
2	
3	
4	
5	
6	
7	
8	

112

INCENTIVE PUBLICATIONS DAILY PRACTICE SERIES
ALGEBRA SKILLS

Numbers & Operations

Skill	1	2	3	4	5	6	7	8	9	10	11	12	13	14	15	16	17	18	19	20	21	22	23	24	25	26	27	28	29	30	31	32	33	34	35	36
Numbers and number systems	√	√	√	√	√																√														√	
Properties of numbers and operations		√				√	√	√	√	√	√	√	√	√			√	√	√	√	√	√	√	√	√	√	√	√	√	√	√	√	√	√		√
Opposites, absolute value, inverses, or reciprocals	√	√	√		√				√				√						√	√	√		√						√							√
Sets, set theory				√						√									√		√					√			√						√	
Factoring (including polynomials)															√	√			√					√	√		√				√		√			
Read, write, compare, order numbers	√	√		√	√	√	√	√	√					√								√				√				√						
Operations with integers	√	√	√	√	√	√	√	√	√	√	√	√	√	√	√	√	√	√	√	√	√	√	√	√	√	√	√	√	√	√	√	√	√	√	√	√
Operations with rational numbers	√	√	√	√	√	√	√	√	√	√	√	√	√	√	√	√	√	√	√	√	√	√	√	√	√	√	√	√	√	√	√	√	√	√	√	√
Operations with exponential numbers or roots	√	√	√	√	√	√	√	√	√	√	√	√	√	√	√	√	√	√	√	√	√	√	√	√	√	√	√	√	√	√	√	√	√	√	√	√
Order of operations	√	√	√	√	√			√																√	√		√		√		√					

The Language of Algebra

Skill	1	2	3	4	5	6	7	8	9	10	11	12	13	14	15	16	17	18	19	20	21	22	23	24	25	26	27	28	29	30	31	32	33	34	35	36
Use or and define terms	√	√	√	√	√	√	√	√	√	√	√	√	√	√	√	√	√	√	√	√	√				√	√			√	√	√	√	√	√	√	√
Identify expressions, equations, and inequalities and their components	√		√				√		√				√		√							√	√		√		√		√	√	√	√	√	√	√	√
Translate words into expressions, equations, or inequalities and vice versa	√	√			√	√	√		√	√	√	√	√	√	√	√	√	√	√		√	√	√	√	√	√			√	√	√	√	√	√	√	√
Simplify expressions	√	√		√	√	√	√			√	√	√	√	√	√	√	√	√	√	√	√	√	√	√	√	√		√	√	√	√	√		√	√	√
Simplify two sides of an equation				√	√						√													√	√	√	√									
Simplify inequalities							√					√	√	√	√	√	√					√				√		√	√			√			√	
Evaluate expressions	√	√	√	√	√	√	√	√	√	√	√	√	√	√	√	√	√	√	√						√	√		√						√		√

113

©Incentive Publications, Inc., Nashville, TN

INCENTIVE PUBLICATIONS DAILY PRACTICE SERIES
ALGEBRA SKILLS

Exponents, Roots, & Radicals

Skill	1	2	3	4	5	6	7	8	9	10	11	12	13	14	15	16	17	18	19	20	21	22	23	24	25	26	27	28	29	30	31	32	33	34	35	36
Expressions with whole number exponents	✓	✓	✓	✓	✓	✓	✓	✓		✓	✓	✓	✓	✓	✓	✓	✓	✓	✓	✓	✓	✓	✓	✓	✓		✓	✓	✓	✓	✓		✓	✓	✓	✓
Scientific notation	✓	✓	✓		✓	✓	✓		✓			✓			✓	✓	✓	✓			✓		✓	✓	✓	✓	✓	✓		✓		✓				
Operations with exponents or roots	✓			✓	✓	✓	✓		✓	✓	✓	✓	✓	✓	✓	✓	✓		✓	✓	✓			✓		✓		✓	✓	✓			✓		✓	✓
Evaluate or simplify expressions with exponents or roots	✓	✓	✓		✓	✓			✓	✓	✓	✓	✓	✓	✓	✓	✓	✓		✓	✓		✓	✓	✓	✓	✓	✓	✓				✓	✓	✓	✓
Negative, fractional, variable, or zero exponents or roots													✓	✓	✓	✓	✓	✓		✓				✓	✓			✓					✓	✓		
Raise a power to a power							✓													✓						✓				✓							✓
Cubes and higher powers				✓	✓	✓	✓	✓	✓	✓	✓	✓	✓	✓	✓	✓	✓	✓	✓	✓					✓	✓	✓	✓	✓				✓	✓	✓	✓
Roots	✓	✓	✓	✓	✓	✓	✓	✓	✓	✓	✓	✓	✓	✓	✓	✓	✓	✓	✓	✓	✓	✓		✓	✓	✓		✓	✓	✓	✓	✓	✓	✓	✓	
Radical expressions	✓	✓	✓	✓	✓	✓	✓	✓	✓	✓	✓	✓	✓	✓	✓	✓	✓	✓	✓	✓	✓	✓	✓						✓	✓	✓	✓	✓	✓	✓	

Solving Equations & Inequalities

Skill	1	2	3	4	5	6	7	8	9	10	11	12	13	14	15	16	17	18	19	20	21	22	23	24	25	26	27	28	29	30	31	32	33	34	35	36
Equations with one variable	✓	✓	✓	✓	✓	✓	✓	✓	✓	✓	✓	✓	✓	✓	✓	✓	✓	✓	✓	✓	✓	✓	✓	✓	✓	✓	✓	✓	✓	✓	✓	✓	✓	✓	✓	✓
Equations with rational numbers	✓	✓	✓	✓	✓	✓	✓	✓	✓	✓	✓	✓	✓		✓	✓	✓	✓	✓		✓	✓		✓	✓	✓	✓	✓	✓	✓	✓	✓	✓	✓	✓	✓
Equations with exponents	✓	✓		✓	✓	✓	✓		✓	✓	✓	✓				✓	✓	✓			✓	✓		✓	✓	✓	✓	✓	✓	✓	✓	✓	✓	✓		✓
Equations with radicals				✓	✓	✓		✓	✓	✓	✓	✓	✓	✓	✓	✓	✓	✓	✓								✓	✓	✓	✓		✓		✓		
Proportions	✓	✓	✓		✓															✓	✓								✓	✓		✓				
Inequalities	✓	✓	✓	✓	✓	✓		✓			✓	✓	✓	✓	✓	✓	✓	✓		✓	✓		✓	✓	✓	✓	✓	✓	✓	✓	✓		✓	✓	✓	✓
Polynomial equations	✓	✓	✓	✓	✓	✓	✓		✓	✓	✓	✓	✓	✓	✓	✓	✓	✓	✓		✓		✓	✓	✓	✓	✓	✓	✓	✓	✓		✓	✓	✓	✓
Identify, solve linear equations	✓	✓	✓	✓	✓	✓	✓		✓		✓	✓	✓	✓	✓	✓	✓	✓	✓	✓	✓	✓	✓	✓	✓	✓	✓	✓	✓	✓	✓	✓	✓	✓	✓	✓
Solve systems of equations	✓	✓	✓		✓	✓								✓		✓	✓						✓	✓	✓	✓	✓	✓	✓			✓	✓	✓	✓	✓
Quadratic formula or equations																						✓	✓	✓	✓	✓	✓				✓	✓	✓	✓	✓	✓
Check accuracy of solutions	✓	✓	✓	✓	✓	✓	✓	✓	✓			✓																✓								✓

114

INCENTIVE PUBLICATIONS DAILY PRACTICE SERIES
ALGEBRA SKILLS

Applications of Algebra

Skill	1	2	3	4	5	6	7	8	9	10	11	12	13	14	15	16	17	18	19	20	21	22	23	24	25	26	27	28	29	30	31	32	33	34	35	36
Choose or write correct equation to solve a problem	✓	✓	✓	✓	✓	✓	✓	✓	✓	✓	✓	✓	✓	✓	✓	✓	✓	✓	✓	✓	✓	✓	✓	✓	✓	✓	✓	✓	✓	✓	✓	✓	✓	✓	✓	
Measurements or measurement units				✓			✓	✓		✓								✓			✓			✓	✓	✓			✓							
Trigonometry																									✓									✓	✓	✓
Pythagorean Theorem			✓					✓			✓								✓	✓			√x					✓	✓	✓		✓			✓	✓
Formulas	✓	✓	✓	✓	✓	✓	✓	✓	✓	✓	✓	✓	✓	✓	✓	✓	✓	✓	✓		✓	✓	✓	✓	✓		✓	✓	✓	✓	✓	✓			✓	✓
Problems with statistical data	✓								✓	✓	✓	✓	✓				✓	✓	✓	✓	✓	✓	✓				✓		✓							
Solve problems with proportions	✓	✓						✓	✓	✓							✓			✓					✓						✓				✓	
Permutations, combinations, and probabilities	✓			✓		✓	✓		✓			✓		✓												✓			✓			✓			✓	
Word problems with integers		✓	✓	✓	✓	✓	✓	✓	✓	✓	✓	✓	✓	✓	✓	✓	✓		✓			✓	✓	✓	✓	✓	✓	✓	✓	✓	✓	✓		✓	✓	✓
Word problems with roots, radicals, or exponents			✓				✓					✓			✓		✓			✓	✓				✓					✓					✓	✓
Word problems with rational numbers		✓	✓			✓	✓		✓	✓			✓	✓			✓	✓	✓		✓			✓	✓			✓	✓				✓	✓		
Logic problems	✓	✓	✓	✓	✓	✓	✓	✓	✓	✓	✓	✓	✓	✓	✓	✓	✓	✓	✓	✓	✓	✓	✓	✓	✓	✓	✓	✓	✓	✓	✓	✓	✓	✓	✓	✓
Problems with percent	✓	✓	✓												✓						✓			✓			✓	✓		✓	✓			✓	✓	
Rate or ratio problems	✓	✓	✓	✓	✓	✓	✓	✓	✓		✓	✓	✓		✓	✓	✓	✓	✓	✓	✓									✓	✓			✓	✓	✓
Problems with mixtures, ages, or jobs	✓				✓						✓			✓				✓				✓	✓	✓		✓		✓	✓	✓					✓	✓
Patterns		✓										✓									✓									✓	✓	✓				✓
Apply algebra to real-life situations	✓	✓	✓	✓	✓	✓	✓		✓		✓					✓	✓	✓	✓	✓	✓	✓	✓	✓	✓		✓	✓		✓	✓	✓			✓	✓
Describe or show problem-solving strategies or processes			✓		✓	✓	✓						✓									✓		✓			✓				✓		✓	✓		

115

© Incentive Publications, Inc., Nashville, TN

INCENTIVE PUBLICATIONS DAILY PRACTICE SERIES
ALGEBRA SKILLS

Lines & Graphing

Skill	1	2	3	4	5	6	7	8	9	10	11	12	13	14	15	16	17	18	19	20	21	22	23	24	25	26	27	28	29	30	31	32	33	34	35	36
Terms related to lines and graphing	✓	✓	✓	✓	✓			✓	✓	✓	✓	✓	✓	✓	✓	✓	✓	✓	✓	✓	✓	✓	✓	✓	✓							✓	✓		✓	
Scatter plots	✓														✓											✓										
Ordered pairs	✓	✓		✓	✓				✓								✓																			
Functions					✓		✓		✓	✓				✓		✓						✓		✓	✓			✓	✓	✓	✓	✓	✓		✓	✓
Recognize features of graph from an equation; write equation from looking at graph				✓						✓							✓		✓				✓					✓			✓		✓		✓	✓
Read graphs of linear equations; identify correct graphs			✓							✓		✓							✓	✓	✓			✓								✓		✓		
Graph linear equations							✓									✓				✓												✓				
Graph systems of equations																✓							✓													
Graph quadratic equations													✓	✓	✓	✓	✓			✓	✓		✓	✓				✓		✓	✓		✓			✓
Slope and intercept of a line													✓	✓	✓	✓	✓			✓				✓	✓	✓		✓	✓		✓					
Write or identify linear equations in slope-intercept, point-slope, and standard forms													✓				✓		✓	✓						✓	✓	✓	✓		✓		✓		✓	
Graphs of parabolas																			✓	✓		✓	✓	✓		✓	✓			✓	✓	✓	✓			
Graph absolute value																									✓									✓		
Read graphs of inequalities; identify correct graphs			✓	✓	✓		✓				✓			✓	✓						✓			✓				✓	✓	✓	✓		✓	✓	✓	✓
Graph simple inequalities				✓	✓	✓	✓		✓		✓	✓	✓											✓				✓	✓	✓		✓			✓	
Graph compound inequalities						✓																							✓	✓					✓	✓

116

Use It! Don't Lose It! IP 613-4

Week 1 (pages 5–7)

MONDAY

1. 2×10^9
2. $x = -5$
3. It is a number sentence in which the expressions on either side of the equal sign have the same value.
4. $-12, -5, -3.1, 0, 0.31, \frac{7}{8}, \sqrt{16}, 2^3, 11.5$
5. 4.55%

TUESDAY

1. the sum of nine and seven times a number OR multiply by seven and add nine
2. rational number
3. $x = 5$
4. x, y, 5, 2
5. a. 15; b. 6

WEDNESDAY

1. two and eighteen hundredths OR two point one eight
2. $14 - n$
3. Add the exponents, keeping the base the same. In symbols, this is: $x^m \cdot x^n = x^{m+n}$
4. no (Correct solution is: y = -16)
5. $\frac{8}{26}$ or $\frac{4}{13}$

THURSDAY

1. a. T   d. F
   b. F   e. T
   c. F   f. F
2. 23
3. −12.012
4. 3
5. Equation: 725 + x = 6x; Solution: 145

FRIDAY

1. −15
2. 177 million
3. n = 5
4.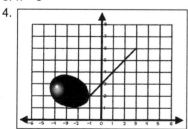
5. Challenge Problem: equation b
   Damon = 8, Brandy = 17; JoJo = 32, Samantha = 40, Will = 24

Week 2 (pages 8–10)

MONDAY

1. x = 600
2. 32
3. 46 − (−387) = 433 ft
4. eighteen multiplied by the difference between a number and another number OR eighteen times the quantity a – b
5. $69,000

TUESDAY

1. b
2. b = 5
3. $4\sqrt{16}$
4. 8000
5. 16%

WEDNESDAY

1. the first one
2. yes
3. d^8
4. find the sum of 12 and 8 (the numbers within the parentheses)
5. $1,750,000

THURSDAY

1. $80,000
2. 5 and −5
3. 3
4. Answers will vary; any number equal to or less than 7.5
5. F, T, T, F, F, F

FRIDAY

1. x = 18
2. distributive
3.
4. Sue would get $60,000.
5.

Week 3 (pages 11–13)

MONDAY

1. $3x - (122 + 9^2) = 514$
2. $\frac{6}{5}$
3. 3^5
4. gnat
5. a. 455; b. 218,400

TUESDAY

1. positive
2. 63
3. $4x + 2y^2$
4. 4 miles
5. 3,429 ft

WEDNESDAY

1. $\frac{1}{4x} = \frac{1}{2}$
2. $16x - x^2 - 16$
3. Subtract the exponent in the denominator from the exponent in the numerator. In symbols: $\frac{x^m}{x^n} = x^{m-n}$
4. $11d^2 - 6 < 40 + d$ *(Although you could simplify further:* $11d^2 - d - 46 < 0$*)*
5. 571,429 hours

THURSDAY

1. yes
2. 60
3. If the stated inequality is ≤ or ≥, the circle is shaded. If the inequality is < or >, the circle is open (not shaded).
4. yes
5. $0.07\mathbf{c} = 4,606,000$

FRIDAY

1. 10
2. r = 60 yrs; t = 20 yrs
3. −900
4. no
5. Challenge Problem: a. 1300; b. 500; c. 2.12×10^5; d. 8.75×10^8; e. 5.29×10^5; f. 8.96×10^5; g. 1.476×10^7; h. 1.645×10^4

Week 4 (pages 14–16)

MONDAY

1. $130,000,000
2. one hundred one and one hundred one ten-thousandths
3. n = −8
4. 4r + 3t
5. (Examples will vary)
   whole numbers (6) – set of non-negative integers
   integers (5 or –5) – whole numbers or their opposites
   rational numbers (0.46 or 3/5) – numbers that can be expressed as a ratio of two integers

ANSWER KEY

irrational numbers (non-repeating and non-terminating decimal or square root of a nonperfect square) – numbers that cannot be written as a ratio of two integers

TUESDAY

1. x = 5 or x = –5
2. 3.53 in OR $\frac{9\pi}{8}$ in
3. –7.7, –7, $\sqrt[3]{-27}$, 0.7, $(-7)^2$, 77
4. 5; 22; 2
5. V = lwh; V = 264 in^3

WEDNESDAY

1. no (Correct measurement is 346 yd)
2. Find the square root of 961
3. l – w = 2.47 OR l – 2.47 = w OR w + 2.47 = l
4. n^{10}
5. twelve years

THURSDAY

1. –6
2. 981
3. 4
4. 513 ft
5. $10^{\frac{1}{2}}$ and π should be placed inside the circle but outside the star; all other numbers are within the star.

FRIDAY

1. no
2. a. R, RA
   b. T, IN, RA
   c. R, N, W, IN, RA
3. h = $\frac{2A}{b + b'}$
4. $\frac{4}{30}$ or $\frac{2}{15}$
5. Challenge Problem:
   The proportion is: $\frac{12}{150} = \frac{x}{2700}$;
   Answer is 216.

Week 5 (pages 17–19)

MONDAY

1. 61,200
2. b = 3
3. 46,656
4. two ($\frac{1}{2}$d and 6d)
5. 2,280,000,000 (or 2.28 billion)

TUESDAY

1. 144, 121, 225, 324
2. $80,000

---

3. The difference between the cube of a number and eighteen is equal to or greater than twenty-five OR x cubed minus eighteen is greater than or equal to twenty-five
4. 1
5. a. 940 ft; b. 112 ft

WEDNESDAY

1. 400,000,000
2. yes
3. $12n = 17 - 3n^3$
4. 4y
5. 1000 mg

THURSDAY

1. 1218
2. –128
3. 24
4. none
5. d

FRIDAY

1. 800%
2. Factors of 48 are 16 and 3. The square root of 16 is 4, but 3 does not have a whole number square root.
3. yes
4.

$3x + y = -4$		
x	y	(x, y)
–5	11	(–5, 11)
–2	2	(–2, 2)
0	–4	(0,–4)
–1	–1	(–1,–1)
1	–7	(1, –7)
3	–13	(3,–13)
5	–19	(5,–19)
6	–22	(6,–22)

5. Challenge Problem:
   25 pounds of each grade

Week 6 (pages 20–22)

MONDAY

1. a. 25; b. 25
2. $9x + 33 + x^2 = 9x + x^2 + 33$ OR any other arrangement of the terms
3. 1.86×10^4
4. x = 9
5. a. 12 hours; b. 111 miles

TUESDAY

1. 1354 ≥ 2j
2. $\frac{1}{2}$
3. Answers will vary: any number equal to or less than 11
4. b = 5 or b = –5

---

5. Equations may vary; one possibility is p + (2p + 8) = 74. Submarine speed is 52 mph; Penguin speed is 22 mph.

WEDNESDAY

1. Add 15
2. about 1644 mph
3. $2 + 4x \geq -2y + 14$ OR $4x + 2y \geq 12$ OR $2x + y \geq 6$
4. In the third step, 3 should be subtracted from the right hand side (not added), leaving –6 rather than 0. The solution would then be p = –1.
5. a. F   b. T   c. F   d. F

THURSDAY

1. 0
2. –1
3. 91.51
4. $3a(b^2 + 3 - 4)$ OR $3a(b^2 - 1)$
5. Circle b, c, e

FRIDAY

1. Expressions may vary; some possibilities: s > t; s = 4t + 8
2. n = 2
3. $\frac{7}{12}$
4. $9xy + x^2y + 45x + 5x^2$
5. Challenge Problem:
   a. 10 p.m. EST;
   b. 1,980 mi;
   c. 1,760 mi;
   d. Explanations will vary.
   (One equation:
   90h + 80h = 3,740
   to yield number of hours
   traveled before trains meet)

Week 7 (pages 23–25)

MONDAY

1. 468 to 39 or $\frac{12}{1}$
2. The cube root of a number is fifteen. OR The cube root of x equals fifteen.
3. 6
4. c = –12
5. 4,900,000

TUESDAY

1. $15x^2 + 2x + 5$
2. 6
3. –2
4. 186 – x – 18 – 25.75 – 30 – 12 = 35.30 (Missing check is 64.95)
5. a. $\frac{24}{60}$ or $\frac{2}{5}$; b. $\frac{23}{59}$

WEDNESDAY

1. $-10 \geq x$, $3x \approx 4y$, $77 < y$
2. $10n^8$
3. 12:55 PM
4. 627
5. no

THURSDAY

1. $4y(x - 3 + 4y)$
2. no
3. $z(2 + w)$ and $w(w + z)$
4.  ($x \geq -4$)
5. c

FRIDAY

1.

x - y = 0		
x	y	(x, y)
-2	-2	(-2,-2)
-1	-1	(-1,-1)
1	1	(1, 1)
2	2	(2,2)

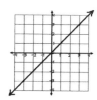

2. 24
3. a. 6; b. 6, c. 36, d. 1
4. -28
5. Challenge Problem: $120

Week 8 (pages 26-28)

MONDAY

1. three: 12, 16, 9
2. $n = 2.5$
3. 10^8 or 100,000,000
4. 10,000
5. $(\frac{1}{4}x)(\frac{1}{5})(57,000,000) = 22,800$
   Answer: 5 shows

TUESDAY

1. $720
2. 23
3. $2x - 5^2 > 12$
4. $p = -8$
5.

10	11	5	8
3	14	4	13
6	7	9	12
15	2	16	1

WEDNESDAY

1. $30x^6y^5$
2. 12, 14, 16
3. $-3b$
4. yes
5. 34 hours and 23 minutes

THURSDAY

1. 20
2. 1
3. $x = 10$
4. $16 - (-68) = 84$ FT
5. Third and fourth statements are true.

FRIDAY

1. 6,650
2. 13 m
3. 6
4. $\frac{3}{8}, \frac{2}{5}, \frac{1}{2}, \frac{\sqrt{16}}{5}, \frac{9}{7}, \frac{6}{3}$
5. Challenge Problem:
   a. $P = \frac{5}{9}$ c. $P = \frac{4}{9}$
   b. $P = \frac{3}{9}$ or $\frac{1}{3}$ d. $P = \frac{1}{72}$

Week 9 (pages 29-31)

MONDAY

1. third choice: $2 (10^4)(1^2)$
2. 6.24×10^9
3. 6
4. $w = 10$
5. b, c

TUESDAY

1. Sentences will vary. Check to make sure answer appropriately demonstrates the Identity Property.
   Example: $5 \cdot 1 = 5$ and $1 \cdot 5 = 5$.
2. b
3. the quantity negative seven plus three times the cube root of three hundred forty-three
4. 4
5. a. $P = \frac{3}{26}$; b. $\frac{23}{26}$; c. $\frac{1}{2600}$ (The answer to c results from doing this: $\frac{3}{26} \cdot \frac{2}{25} \cdot \frac{1}{14} = \frac{1}{2600}$)

WEDNESDAY

1. no
2. $-3x^5$
3. 0.002 sq meter
4. $4b^2$ and $2b^2$, $3c$ and $6c$
5. 2.254 ft^3

THURSDAY

1. 2

WEDNESDAY

2. yes
3. $n - 28$
4. $-\frac{1}{8}$; $\frac{1}{3}x$; $\frac{1}{x-2}$; $\frac{4}{5}$; $\frac{-5}{x}$; $\frac{3}{10}$
5. a (Solution is: 14 days)

FRIDAY

1. 2100%
2. subtract 16
3. $\frac{10c}{d}$
4. ($x < 5$)
5. Challenge Problem:
   a. 1.59 ft/sec   d. 19.5 sec
   b. 65 sec   e. 4.2 ft/sec
   c. 36.5 ft   f. 1258 mi

Week 10 (pages 32-34)

MONDAY

1. 30 hours
2. one
3. $15\sqrt{3}$
4. $\sqrt{7} \sqrt{10}$
5. about 6522

TUESDAY

1. 0
2. 159
3. -22
4. Thirty-five is the sum of a number and negative two times another number. OR Thirty-five equals p plus the quantity negative two q.
5. Numbers in A (but not in B) = $-6, \frac{2}{3}, -30, 8, \sqrt[3]{-64}$
   Numbers in B (but not in A) = $-8, -\frac{1}{2}, -3, 5.44$
   Numbers in intersection of A and B = $\frac{1}{2}, 6.75, 4^2$

WEDNESDAY

1. $62y + 2$
2. 11 kg
3. $6w^8$
4. b
5. 15.9 mph

THURSDAY

1. $2 \cdot 2 \cdot 7$
2. $x \geq 6$
3. $x = 3$
4. $\frac{4}{5}(1080) - 17 = \frac{1}{2}b$
5. 49,000

FRIDAY

1. no

ANSWER KEY

2. $6y^3 + 6xy - 18xz$
3. 208.8 kg (The missing score was 200 kg)
4. yes
5. Challenge Problem: a. 0.00000001; b. 4; c. 3.56×10^5; d. 256; e. 11; f. 0.05; g. 11^3

Week 11 (pages 35–37)

MONDAY
1. $169.00
2. $10y$
3. c
4. $\frac{1}{x^5}$; $\frac{1}{6^3}$ or $\frac{1}{216}$; $\frac{1}{(4 \cdot 3)^2}$ or $\frac{1}{36}$
5. The suspect who is 6 feet tall (Sue)

TUESDAY
1. $x = 320$
2. Answers may vary: $75 < m < 99$
3. 3
4. 2:15 a.m.
5. $ 82,226,474

WEDNESDAY
1. 11.5 hrs
2. $6\frac{2}{3}x - 5 = 75$
3. 20,000
4. $24x$
5. no

THURSDAY
1. 92
2. 0
3. no
4. $9x$
5. a. 22 weeks; b. yes; c. 52.5

FRIDAY
1. 14.5 or $14\frac{1}{2}$
2. Correct graph is b: shows $x \le 5$.
3. $n > -32$
4. 200
5. Challenge Problem:
   A. There may be more than one correct answer. One possibility is: 55–100s, 22–50s, 100–5s
   B. There may be more than one correct answer. One possibility is: 80 quarters, 120 dimes, 5–50 cent pieces
   C. $37,870; $393
   D. $8,000
   E. $197,760
   F. $22,262

Week 12 (pages 38–40)

MONDAY
1. $-272°$ C
2. Seventeen is greater or equal to the difference between a number squared and negative one. OR, Seventeen is greater than or equal to x squared minus a negative one.
3. 27 days
4. $\frac{1}{x^3}$
5. c, d, f

TUESDAY
1. $136.4 - (-128) = 264.4°$
2. >
3. a number squared divided by the product of that number and another number OR, c squared divided by c times d
4. the third choice
5. 0.8 ft^3

WEDNESDAY
1. 100 seconds or 1 min, 40 sec
2. n^7
3. 24th
4. no
5. a. $P = \frac{185}{360}$ or $\frac{37}{72}$;
   b. $P = \frac{265}{360}$ or $\frac{53}{72}$;
   c. $P = \frac{270}{360}$ or $\frac{3}{4}$

THURSDAY
1. natural, counting, whole, real, integer, rational
2. 6
3.
   ![number line](x ≥ 6)
   ($x \ge 6$)
4. $x - (y + 7)$ OR $x - y - 7$
5. Equation for total is: $7x - 16 - 754$; Joe's distance $x = 110$ ft; Moe is $2x$; Flo is $x - 16$, Zoe is $1\frac{1}{2}(3x)$

FRIDAY
1. 120
2. 3
3. $y > \frac{2}{3}$
4. yes
5. Challenge Problem:
   A: $x = -y$; B. $y = 2x + 1$;
   C. $y = x + 2$; D. $y = -x + 3$;
   E. $x - 3 = y$

Week 13 (pages 41–43)

MONDAY
1. 930
2. -16
3. c, e, f
4. $x = 10.7$
5. a. .08 ounces per second; b. 125 seconds or 2 min, 5 sec; c. six

TUESDAY
1. no
2. the first one
3. $\sqrt[3]{216} \ge x + \sqrt{9}$
4. $x = 4$, $x = -6$
5. more

WEDNESDAY
1. Approx 77,848 g
2. $-8x^4$
3. c
4. $10n - 10 = 3n + 4$
5. $\frac{100}{9}$ or 100:9

THURSDAY
1. 3,040 ounces
2. $7x$
3. a. -42; b. $\frac{-1}{12}$; c. 96
4. To find slope from the graph: Choose two points on the line. Count the vertical distance (rise) and the horizontal distance (run) between the two points. Then divide the rise by the run to determine slope.
5. 49 seconds

FRIDAY
1.

FRACTION	DECIMAL	PERCENT
$\frac{7}{8}$	0.875	87.5%
$\frac{9}{25}$	0.36	36%
$\frac{1}{5}$	0.2	20%
$\frac{3}{25}$	0.12	12%
$\frac{4}{5}$	0.8	80%
$1\frac{3}{10}$	1.3	130%

2. It is not linear because it contains variables raised to a power greater than one.
3. $x = 4$ or $x = \frac{-8}{3}$
4. $x \le -\frac{1}{2}$;
   ![number line]

5. Challenge Problem:
   a. John ate 35 per hour. Ben ate 15 per hour.
   b. The total time was 6 hours.

Week 14 (pages 44–46)

MONDAY
1. 110 ft
2. $\frac{2}{9}$
3. b, c
4. 12
5. a: 1,132; b: 1,031 ft; c: 377

TUESDAY
1. –14
2. $x^3 - 3y = 77$
3. no
4. a. 1027; b. –3x; c. $7\sqrt{3}$
5. 7.8 ft^3

WEDNESDAY
1. $\frac{2}{3}$
2. no
3. $y \geq 2x^2 + 10x + 10$
4. second one: $6p^6q$
5. a. 13.7m; b. $\frac{6}{26}$ or $\frac{3}{13}$

THURSDAY
1. 155 ft^2
2. $12\sqrt{2}$
3. $\frac{13}{60}$
4. $(x + y)^2$
5. a. 0.07 ounces; b. $\frac{10}{24}$ or $\frac{5}{12}$

FRIDAY
1. day 49
2. Slope = 3; y-intercept = 4
3. x = –4
4. T, T, T, F
5. Challenge Problem:
   Perimeter: hourglass, burger, yo-yo, bonfire, drum, beach towel;
   Area: hourglass, burger, yo-yo, bonfire, drum, beach towel

Week 15 (pages 47–49)

MONDAY
1. 2624.67 ft
2. no (Correct would be $x^5 + 1$)
3. the product of a number squared and the square root of twelve OR x squared times the square root of twelve
4. x = 0
5. a. 2.7 min; b. 45 hours

TUESDAY
1. 10
2. a, d

3. $x \geq -2$
4. 52
5. 14,100

WEDNESDAY
1. 2×10^6
2. $(q - 2)$
3. 36 in^2
4. two: $8x^2$ and $-x^2$
5. pencil: 1795; laptop: 1987

THURSDAY
1. $262
2. 88, 92, 106
3. 1, $\frac{1}{64}$, 12, $\frac{1}{25}$
4. $3b^4 + 7b^2 + 2b + 2$
5. 20%

FRIDAY
1. yes (x < 8)

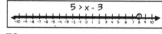

2. 72
3. slope = 0.6; y-intercept –0.5
4.

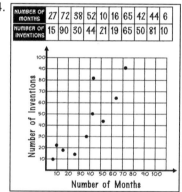

5. Challenge Problem: zipper: 1917; paper: 105; DVD: 1995; dishwasher: 1886; Velcro: 1948; magnifying glass: 1250; helicopter: 1939; pop top can: 1963; cell phone: 1979

Week 16 (pages 50–52)

MONDAY
1. 320
2. 18
3. $-2n + 2y$
4. 14%
5. four minutes

TUESDAY
1. a
2. $9a^4b^3$
3. w = h + 3   OR   h = w – 3
4. $-\frac{2}{5}$

5. y = 2x – 3

WEDNESDAY
1. 24x + 2
2. 6401 m
3. 64
4. d
5. 5 m

THURSDAY
1. –6 a
2. 6.73×10^{-4}
3. –4p – 1
4. 18,000
5. In 2007: 129; in 2008: 136

FRIDAY
1. 61,000 g
2. $x \geq -1$
3. $\frac{1}{2}$
4. $3xy(y + 2xy - 1)$
5. Challenge Problem:
   a. Table (1, –2); (3, 2); (0, –4);
   b.
   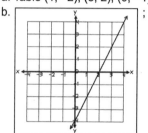
   c. Explanation: the solution is the x-intercept of the graph;
   d. solution: x = 2

Week 17 (pages 53–55)

MONDAY
1. 2000^2 OR 4×10^6
2. $4x^{-3}y^5$
3. 2x – y = –6
4. (6, 4)
5. no

TUESDAY
1. Multiply 7 times p and 7 times 6.
2. b
3. b
4. 66.25
5. 884,260 ft^2

WEDNESDAY
1. second choice
2. 25
3. a
4. $-4a^2 - 36$ OR $-4(a^2 + 9)$
5. 1260 a day

ANSWER KEY

THURSDAY

1. $(10^4)(14.2)$
2. $b^2 + c + a^2b = c + b^2 + a^2b$ OR any other order of the three terms
3. $x = \frac{36}{13}$
4. The solution is $x > 3$;
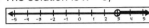
5. a. 51; b. 44; c. 110; d. 16

FRIDAY

1. a. $m = 7$; b. $n = 154$
2. 192
3. yes
4. 1.32×10^9
5. Challenge Problem: The riddle of the sphinx is: a person. When a person is young, they crawl on all fours. When they're in the prime of life, they walk on two legs. When they are old (evening), they walk with a cane. Challenge Problem: $h = 450$ ft.

Week 18 (pages 56–58)

MONDAY

1. 8.5 mg
2. $\frac{1}{x^3}$
3. $n - m$
4. no
5. 957

TUESDAY

1. 811,840
2. $x^{\frac{1}{2}}$; $12^{\frac{1}{3}}$;
3. $6x - 4(y + 3)$
4. 10
5. a. 4.2×10^6 d. 2×10^6
   b. 1×10^{-6} e. 1×10^{11}
   c. 5×10^8 f. 2.3×10^9

WEDNESDAY

1. $(ab)(a^2 + b - 3)$
2. negative three times the cube root of x
3. $6x^3y$
4. 576
5. a. Answers will vary, depending on the date. If the days were calculated to the end of 2006, the total would be 11,588.
   b. Allowing for 72 leap years in the 288 year period, the fine would be $5259.60.

THURSDAY

1. yes
2. $2x^4 - y^6$

---

3. $-\frac{9}{2}$
4. $n = \frac{4}{7}$
5. 285,714,286

FRIDAY

1. 29
2. $2x^2y$
3. no
4. $(-1, 2)$; $(-4, 0)$; $(1, -3)$
5. Challenge Problem: 60 pounds of pure chocolate

Week 19 (pages 59–61)

MONDAY

1. 4.9 ft^2
2. x
3. a. 2; b. 1
4. $y = 2x + 11$
5. 500 ft

TUESDAY

1. x^3
2. $2c^2(c^4 - 2c + 3)$
3. x-intercept is 4; y-intercept is 12
4. $V = 6x^3y^3z$
5. 40 days

WEDNESDAY

1. $84,000
2. yz
3. $\{1, 7\}$
4. $\frac{3}{8}$ hour or $22\frac{1}{2}$ min
5. a. $y = 4$; b. $x = 3$

THURSDAY

1. six-2's; four-5's; and one-11
2. ab^4
3. $24x^3yzw$
4. $|x - 4| \le 2$
5. 1.375×10^{10} dollars

FRIDAY

1. 599%
2. yes
3. 10 in, 15 in, 12 in, 12 in
4. $\frac{3}{4}$
5. Challenge Problem: 30

Week 20 (pages 62–64)

MONDAY

1. 34.32 seconds
2. 3^4
3. right triangles
4. 84.9 miles

5.
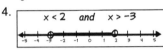

TUESDAY

1. x^{15}
2. 13
3. $\frac{2}{3}$
4.
$$x < 2 \quad and \quad x > -3$$
5. $-.129$

WEDNESDAY

1. 80 mph
2. yes
3. about 42 mph
4. $\{1, 4, 6, 7, 8, 9\}$
5. a

THURSDAY

1. 147 ft/sec
2. $\frac{1}{27}$
3. 4
4. b
5. 4.6 seconds

FRIDAY

1. 1
2. $x = 8, y = 2$
3. 21.4 mph
4.
5. Challenge Problem:
   A. Heartstop Drop = -3;
   B. Easy Street = 0;
   C. Sunshine Avenue = -1;
   D. Last Chance Run = $-\frac{2}{9}$;
   E. Rainbow Canyon = -2;
   F. Home Stretch = $-\frac{1}{4}$

Week 21 (pages 65–67)

MONDAY

1. 210 meters
2. $\frac{y^2}{x^2}$
3. T equals P times the quantity one plus i raised to the nth.
4. b
5. a. 1,010 ft; b. 5,017 ft

TUESDAY

1. greater
2. 18,500 ft
3. one
4. $3207.17
5. 40,115

WEDNESDAY

1. 10 inches in diameter
2. true
3. the y coordinate of a point where a graph crosses the y-axis
4. $x < -\frac{5}{2}$
5. 1= c; 2 = b; 3 = d; 4 = a

THURSDAY

1. $\frac{48.77}{50}$ OR 98% of the pool
2. $81 - 16\,x^4$
3. 1.89×10^4 ft
4. a. z^3 in^3; b. $27z^3$ in^3
5. a. 96; b. 24,576

FRIDAY

1. A = xy; P = 2(x + y) or 2x + 2y
2. a. $\frac{1}{13}$; b. $\frac{2}{13}$
3. 30 ft, 35 ft, 55 ft
4. 20,000 ft^3
5. Challenge Problem: $2000\sqrt{2}$ ft

Week 22 (pages 68–70)

MONDAY

1. 11,097
2. 1728
3. −3
4. 181 ft
5. a.

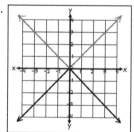

;

   b. The negative sign creates a mirror image of |x| and the line of reflection is the x-axis.

TUESDAY

1. approximately $1136 per card
2. c
3. up
4. a. y = (x + 3) (x − 4);
   b. x = −3 and x = 4
5. 3,585 lbs ; Explanations will vary, but student should mention exponential decay and the

formula for finding it.

WEDNESDAY

1. 220
2. x = 11 and x = 31
3. growth
4.

5. a. 1482 bags; b. 43 countries

THURSDAY

1. 3,728
2. $6x^2 - x - 15$
3. 2
4. 9.4
5. 1439 ducks; 5100 gum pack.

FRIDAY

1. 4.39×10^5
2. x = 2
3. down
4. no; An absolute value can never be negative.
5. Challenge Problem: a. 6 years; b. about $4\frac{1}{2}$ years

Week 23 (pages 71–73)

MONDAY

1. $2,939 billion
2. x = 8, x = −2
3. −4
4. 2.1 square feet
5. a.

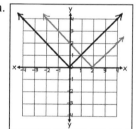

;

   b. It shifts (translates) the original function two units to the right

TUESDAY

1. Round to $388,000,000; 3.88×10^8
2. $\frac{3}{x^2y^4}$
3. a. y = (x + 5) (x − 4)
   b. x = −5 and x = 4
4. up
5. Japan $10.80 (in U.S. dollars) and India = $.20 (U.S.)

WEDNESDAY

1. 1,530,350
2. (x + 2) (x + 3)

3. b
4. a.

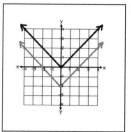

;

   b. It causes the graph to shift two units down (vertical translation)
5. Julie earns $8 an hour; Hank earns $6 an hour.

THURSDAY

1. Gloria was 87 and Jackie was 9.
2. $4x^2 + 4x - 8$
3. zero
4.

5. 10 pounds of the $1.20 popcorn grade and 25 pounds of the $1.80 grade

FRIDAY

1. $\frac{3}{8}$ hour or 22.5 min
2. down
3. $7\sqrt{2}$
4. approximately .06545 in^3
5. Challenge Problem: Across: 5. null set; 6. hypotenuse; 8. binomial; 10. median; 11. counterexample; 12. variable; 13. integers; 14. parallel
   Down: 1. slope; 2. as the crow flies; 3. rational number; 4. equation; 7. real numbers; 9. quadrant; 10. mode

Week 24 (pages 74–76)

MONDAY

1. 13.9 tons
2. $7x^2(5 + 2)$
3. prime number
4. $z = \frac{(x + y)}{a^2b^2}$
5. a. 5,207,276 km; b. about $.26

TUESDAY

1. 2.44×10^6 m
2. four-ninths
3. exponential decay
4. $f = \frac{E}{h}$
5. 5.865696×10^{12} miles; descriptions will vary (dimensional analysis is preferable)

ANSWER KEY

WEDNESDAY

1. about 3.9×10^2
2. $x^2 + 2xy + y^2$
3. x^n
4.
5. c

THURSDAY

1. 720
2. $(x + y)(x - y)$
3. b
4. $25 - 50s + 25s^2$
5. a. 22.1 lb; b. .17 lb

FRIDAY

1. about 8.8×10^5
2. $m_2 = \dfrac{Fd^2}{gm_1}$
3. $\dfrac{1}{v^{16}}$
4. $xyz^6 - xy$
5. Challenge Problem:
   a. 1375 kg/m^3; b. more; c. more; explanations will vary but should include this idea: It is more dense than water, so it should be more dense than air.

Week 25 (pages 77–79)

MONDAY

1. 102 ft
2. yes
3. M = multiplication; D = division
4.
5. 29,982.2° C

TUESDAY

1. 49.9% (in a non leap year)
2. 9a
3. distributive property of multiplication over subtraction
4. $y = 0$
5. $.0815 \text{ lb/ft}^3$

WEDNESDAY

1. 2.2 lb
2. $2^3 \cdot 2^6 = 2^9$
3. yes
4. $x = -3$
5. baby = 2 mi; pickles = 25 mi

THURSDAY

1. approximately 39 ft
2. 6.3×10^7
3. 0

---

4. $z = 1200$
5. 15 minutes

FRIDAY

1. 56 mi
2. $(x - 3)(x + 6)$
3.
4. $w \cdot (42 - w)$
5. Challenge Problem:
   a. Beirut;
   b. parabola;
   c. zero;
   d. 3.8 in;
   e. March – April

Week 26 (pages 80–82)

MONDAY

1. 1.49 ft
2. $9a^2 + 6ab + b^2$
3. all the elements from both sets
4. $2x + 3y = 1$
5. 8,000 miles and 17,000 banana-related objects

TUESDAY

1. 35,000
2. m
3. $2 \cdot 5 \cdot 5$
4. $6x^2 - 5xy + y^2$
5. .6124

WEDNESDAY

1. x = eggs crushed = 13
2. $\dfrac{x^{-4}}{y^6}$ or $\dfrac{1}{x^4 y^6}$
3. base
4. $y = \dfrac{3}{2}x + 2$
5. 32,786

THURSDAY

1. $t = \sqrt{\dfrac{2d}{g}}$
2. $xy^3 z$
3. $y = -\dfrac{1}{2}x - 6$
4. $(a - b)(a - b)$
5. 8, 75

FRIDAY

1. $wk - 23$
2. $(a + b)(a + b)$
3. yes
4. a
5. Challenge Problem:
   a. $2500 - 2w$
   b. $w(2500 - 2w)$
   c. $w(2500 - 2w) \geq 50,000$

Week 27 (pages 83–85)

MONDAY

1. a. 37,843,200; b. 2,724,710,400
2. $(3x - 4)(x + 3)$
3. interest
4. a. 110; b. 220; c. approx 42%
5. about 6 ft

TUESDAY

1. 3.67 ft^2
2. $x = 0$; $x = 18$
3. exponent
4. c
5. a. 3,027,456 l
   b. about 800,000 gal

WEDNESDAY

1. 206
2. $x = 10$; $x = 0$
3. a trinomial
4. 2400 ft^2
5. A = 13,000 ml/min
   B = 12,900 ml/min

THURSDAY

1. a. 94,535,000; b. 99,905,465,000
2. binomial
3. For any real number r:
   $r \cdot 0 = 0 \cdot r = 0$
4. a, d
5. a. 2.03 m^2; b. 20.3 mg

FRIDAY

1. $-y - 8$
2. $\dfrac{1}{8}x = 15$; $x = 120$ g
3. $x = 2$; $x = 3$
4. b
5. Challenge Problem:
   a. P = .31; b. P = .69; c. P = .13;
   d. P = .107; e. P = .095

Week 28 (pages 86–88)

MONDAY

1. 2.25×10^7
2. $\dfrac{x + 2}{x - 1}$
3. $y = 2x + 7$
4. Gretzky = 894; Pele = 1,280
5. b

TUESDAY

1. 18
2. $+4, -4$
3. no
4. $y = 33$
5. a. $x + 1.75x = 80,850,000$
   b. $29,400,000

WEDNESDAY

1. 1548
2. x^7y^3
3. yes
4. c
5. 22.2%

THURSDAY

1. 24%
2. 381.51 in^3 (using π = 3.14)
3. yes
4. a. Pythagorean Theorem; b. no
5. d

FRIDAY

1. a. 254.34 in^2 (using π = 3.14) ;
   b. about 31,030
2. x = 3
3. $4x^2 - 16$
4. x = 4; x = –2
5. Challenge Problem:
   Palace = 22,076;
   United Center = 21,711;
   Madison Square Garden = 19,763

Week 29 (pages 89–91)

MONDAY

1. x = 400
2. $6x^2y(x+ 4 + 2x^3y)$
3. whole numbers, irrational numbers, rational numbers, integers (whole numbers optional); Examples will vary. Check for accuracy.
4. $(\frac{7}{2}, 4)$
5. a. P = $\frac{1}{20}$ or 5%;
   b. P = $\frac{19}{20}$ or 95%;
   c. P = 0;
   d. P = $\frac{3}{20}$ or 15%;
   e. P = $\frac{9}{20}$ or 45%;
   Bonus: $\frac{1}{16}$ or 6.25%

TUESDAY

1. x = 4 seconds; y = 5
2. (x − 7) (x + 8) x = 7; x = –8
3. a. a proportion; b. cross multiply; c. x = $\frac{30}{7}$ or 4.28571
4. $\sqrt{(c - a)^2 + (d - b)^2}$ or
   $\sqrt{(a - c)^2 + (b - d)^2}$

5. You'll need a square that is 12 inches on each side to allow for folding the edges into a box.

WEDNESDAY

1. prime
2. $x\sqrt{7}$
3. d
4. $y = -\frac{1}{3}x - \frac{4}{3}$
5. 6%

THURSDAY

1. $|x - 2000| \le 2$
2. 343 units^2
3. integers ≤ 0
4. –4 < x < 2 OR
   x < 2 AND x > –4
5. a. 14.13 in^3; b. 21.20 in^3

FRIDAY

1. x = 29
2. c
3.

Sentences	Equation (yes or no?)	Formula (yes or no?)
$A = \pi r^2$	yes	yes
$2a > 0$	no	no
$V = \frac{4}{3}\pi r^3$	yes	yes
$\|x - y\| = 2$	yes	no

4. $C = \frac{F - 32}{1.8}$
5. Challenge Problem: P = .95 or $\frac{95}{100}$; Explanations will vary. (One possibility is use of this equation: $P(A \cup B) = P(A) + P(B) - P(A \cap B)$ = .65 + .70 − .40 = .95)

Week 30 (pages 92–94)

MONDAY

1. t = $\sqrt{2}$ sec
2. 3
3. x = 5 ± $\sqrt{2}$
4. $a = -\frac{2}{3}b$
5. b; x = 2,000,000

TUESDAY

1. 34%
2. $8\sqrt{2}$
3. false (The absolute value of zero is not positive.)
4. V = .25x + .1y + .05z
5. a. Check to see that student has created a graph with solid dots at 160 and 180, and with solid line connecting them;
   b. $|x - 170| = 10$; solution: x = 160, x = 180

WEDNESDAY

1. 87
2. x = –8; x = 2
3. a. 3 (HH, HT, TT)
   b. 4 (HT, TH, TT, HH)
4. 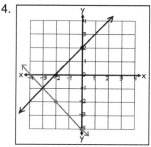 ;
   Solution: (−3, −1)
5. 6 liters

THURSDAY

1. 3
2. a. $x^{a + b - c}$; b. x^a; c. x^b
3. $\frac{1}{3}$ r
4. $\sqrt{.02}$, $\frac{9}{100}$, .067, .05321, 4.55 x 10^{-2}
5. $\frac{3}{4}$ hr going out and 1 hr returning; distance = 30 mi

FRIDAY

1. 13,350
2. $2\sqrt{5}$
3. $A = \frac{1}{2}x^2$
4. 199
5. Challenge Problem:
   a. noon = 8,000;
      4:00 pm = 128,000
   b. A wise opinion is "today".

Week 31 (pages 95–97)

MONDAY

1. 13 in
2. $r = \sqrt{\frac{V}{\pi h}}$
3. $y = (-\frac{1}{2})x + 5.5$
4. If $ax^2 + bx + c = 0$ and $a \ne 0$, then $x = \frac{-b \pm \sqrt{b^2 - 4ac}}{2a}$
5. height (x) = 7 in; length (y) = 13 in

TUESDAY

1. 220
2. $\frac{x\sqrt{x}}{5\sqrt{2}}$ or $\frac{x}{10}\sqrt{2x}$
3. $-\frac{3}{2}$
4. no root
5. 50 times the shuttle

ANSWER KEY

WEDNESDAY

1. 10 ft
2. a. (0, 0); b. y-axis; c. a > 0 opens up; a < 0 opens down
3. $x = \frac{3}{2}$ and $x = -4$
4. $x^2 - x$
5. 3, 17, 5, 13, 7

THURSDAY

1. 45
2. $5\sqrt{2}$
3. true
4. $a = \sqrt{c^2 - b^2}$
5. a. yes; b. 17 jumps

FRIDAY

1. .087 in
2. equal, in proportion
3. $2^n + 1$
4. $x = \frac{2 \pm \sqrt{56}}{2}$
5. Challenge Problem:
   a. 3 seconds; b. 3 meters; c. yes

Week 32 (pages 98–100)

MONDAY

1. 8.21 mi
2. 35
3. a. the set of all possible values of f(x)
   b. the set of all possible values for the first variable
4. $y = -\frac{1}{2}x + \frac{3}{2}$
5. a. 273°K
   b. 263°K
   c. 283°K
   d. −460°F

TUESDAY

1. 4.63 mi^2
2. $\frac{5}{4}$
3. all real numbers ≥ 3
4. $\frac{5}{2}$
5. 87,780,000 J

WEDNESDAY

1. 5500°C
2. 3; 1; 0; $\frac{1}{4}$
3. a. $\frac{-4 \pm \sqrt{76}}{6}$
   b. a = 3, b = 4, c = −5

4.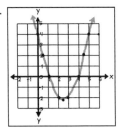

   + solution: x = 1, x = 4
5. x = 136°F, y = −128.6°F

THURSDAY

1. 100,000%
2. a. 8; b. 3; c. 1
3. equal, equal
4. 49
5. .43 hr or 26 min

FRIDAY

1. a.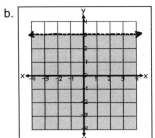

   b.

2. all real numbers except 1
3. a. 17,520 bulbs;
   b. 1.0512×10^6 watts
4. (4a + 3) (3a + 4)
5. Challenge Problem:
   a. 3.2×10^{15} tons of TNT
   b. 1.6×10^{11} bombs

Week 33 (pages 101–103)

MONDAY

1. 1.35 hr or 1 hr, 21 min
2. a. w^4; b. $\frac{1}{w^{\frac{1}{2}}}$ c. w^8; d. $\frac{8w^6}{27}$
3. c
4. x = 2; x = 5
5. 75 Sunday, 300 weekday

TUESDAY

1. 389.567 in^2
2. $\frac{4a^2 - 5a + 2}{2}$
3. yes
4. 36 sq. units
5. w = 3035; x = 24; y = 1097; z = 169

WEDNESDAY

1. $.92 \text{ in}^2$
2. $x^2 + 6x$
3. x-axis: y = 0; y-axis: x = 0
4.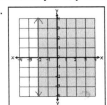

5. a. $P = \frac{2}{3}$; b. $P = \frac{1}{3}$

THURSDAY

1. 62 inches
2. $\frac{3 + 6z}{2x}$
3. $\sin A = \frac{a}{c}$
4. a. first; b. second; c. third
5.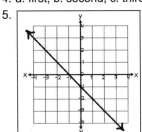

x	y
−1	0
0	−1
1	−2
2	−3

FRIDAY

1. a. 363 in^3; b. no
2. x = 25
3. $y = -\frac{1}{5}x + 2$
4. a. x + 4 > 10; 10 + 4 > x;
   x + 10 > 4
   b. x > 6; x < 14; x > −6; c. 6; d. 14
5. Challenge Problem: a. 36;
   b. $P = \frac{1}{2}$; c, $P = \frac{2}{3}$; d. $P = \frac{1}{6}$

Week 34 (pages 104–106)

MONDAY

1. a. b + r = 30   c. x + 6
   b. a = c + 12   d. e = 15 − x
2. true
3. $\frac{2\sqrt{3}}{3}$
4. Susan is 15; Blake is 5.

5.

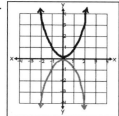

TUESDAY

1. 4.5 yrs
2. $\dfrac{\sqrt{5}}{\sqrt{5}}$
3. $\dfrac{b}{c}$
4. y = 16
5. a. 5,730 yrs   c. 17,190 yrs
   b. 11,460 yrs   d. 22,920 yrs

WEDNESDAY

1. George (x) was 87;
   Peggy was 15
2. x^3
3. true
4. a = $\sqrt{3}$; c = 2
5. one traveled at 5 miles a day; the other traveled at 7 miles a day

THURSDAY

1. j = 6s; j + 2 = 10(s – 3)
2. a. no; b. yes
3. xy = 16 or y = $\dfrac{16}{x}$
4. $\sqrt{x^5}$
5. Sara is 15 and Krista is 10

FRIDAY

1. 1875
2. a = 6; c = $6\sqrt{2}$
3. (3a + 5) (2a – 6)
4. a. T; b. T; c. F
5. Challenge Problem:

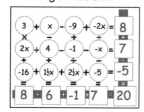

Week 35 (pages 107–109)

MONDAY

1. $628.89
2. domain = {3, 4, 5, 6};
   range = {2, 3, 4}

---

3. slope = $-\dfrac{2}{3}$; x-intercept = $\dfrac{9}{2}$
4. x = 9.4
5. a. $22,750; b. $11,830

TUESDAY

1. x – 6.50 < 20 or x < 26.50
2. a
3. 2x + y = 4
4. solution: x ≥ –2;

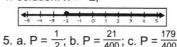

5. a. P = $\dfrac{1}{2}$; b. P = $\dfrac{21}{400}$; c. P = $\dfrac{179}{400}$

WEDNESDAY

1. 8,334
2. a. a^{c-d}; b. z^m
3. y = 24
4. x = 21
5. 5 hrs, 35 min or 5.58 hrs

THURSDAY

1. x < 10; x > 4
2. $37,100
3. y^9
4. a. domain = all real numbers;
   range = all real numbers;
   b. domain = all real numbers,
   range = all non-negative numbers
5. a. a 72-year old
   b. 204.4 per 50 million miles driven
   c. minimum is 46 (safest)

FRIDAY

1. 3887
2. $9\sqrt{2} + 8\sqrt{5}$
3. b
4. 25 in
5. Challenge Problem: x ≥ 0 ; y ≥ 0;
   x ≤ 4; y ≤ 4

Week 36 (pages 110–112)

MONDAY

1. yes, day 27
2. domain: all real numbers;
   range: all real numbers > 0
3. $4a^2 - 4ab + b^2$
4. a. y = –x + $\dfrac{5}{2}$; b. –1; c. $\dfrac{5}{2}$
5. F = $33\dfrac{1}{3}$ N/m

TUESDAY

1. 133.33 min or 2 hrs, 13.33 min

---

2. a. an angle; b. (0, 2)
3. power of a quotient
4.

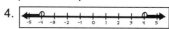

5. a. 12:09 p.m;
   b. Corvette travels 139.3 mi;
   Porsche travels 160.7 mi.

WEDNESDAY

1. a, d
2. n = $\dfrac{PV}{RT}$
3. x = –15; x = 9
4. a. A = πr^2; b. $16r^2$; c. $16r^2 - \pi r^2$
5. $36\dfrac{2}{3}$ liters

THURSDAY

1. a. $\dfrac{2}{7}$ oz; b. 2.7 oz
2. distributive property
3. no
4. 19 yd
5.

FRIDAY

1. $T_0 = T_1 - \dfrac{H}{KA}$
2. (x – yw) (x + yw)
3. m
4. 48.3 ft
5. Challenge Problem:
   a. approx. 5.5 ft;
   b. table: reading right-hand
   column from top to bottom:
   500;
   250;
   166.66 repeating or $166\dfrac{2}{3}$;
   125;
   100;
   83.33 repeating or $83\dfrac{1}{3}$;
   71.43;
   62.5
   c. 500
   d. inverse